RENO

TRAVEL GUIDE 2024

A Comprehensive Travel Guide to the Biggest Little City in the World, Unveiling Hidden Gems, Cultural Delights, and Thrilling Adventures for Every Traveler

BONUS

(TRAVEL ESSENTIALS)

MARVIN JACKSON

WELCOME

Wander through the heart of the city and discover its vibrant arts scene, eclectic boutiques, and historic landmarks.

Experience the excitement of Reno's famous casinos, where you can try your hand at a variety of games, from slots to poker.

Take advantage of Reno's proximity to stunning natural landscapes by embarking on outdoor adventures.

Check out the city's calendar of events for live music performances, art festivals, cultural celebrations, and more.

Prologue:

In the heart of the American West lies a city unlike any other. Nestled at the foot of the majestic Sierra Nevada mountains, Reno beckons travelers with its unique blend of urban sophistication and rugged natural beauty. Known affectionately as the "Biggest Little City in the World," Reno boasts a rich tapestry of history, culture, and adventure waiting to be discovered.

As you embark on a journey through the bustling streets and serene landscapes of Reno, prepare to be captivated by its vibrant energy, diverse communities, and boundless opportunities for exploration. From the glitz and glamour of its famous casinos to the tranquil shores of the Truckee River, each corner of this dynamic city offers a new and exciting experience.

Join us as we delve into the heart of Reno, uncovering its hidden gems, celebrating its cultural heritage, and embracing the spirit of adventure that defines this extraordinary destination. Whether you're a first-time visitor or a seasoned traveler, Reno promises to enchant, inspire, and leave an indelible mark on your soul.

Welcome to Reno: where adventure awaits at every turn, and the possibilities are as endless as the Nevada sky.

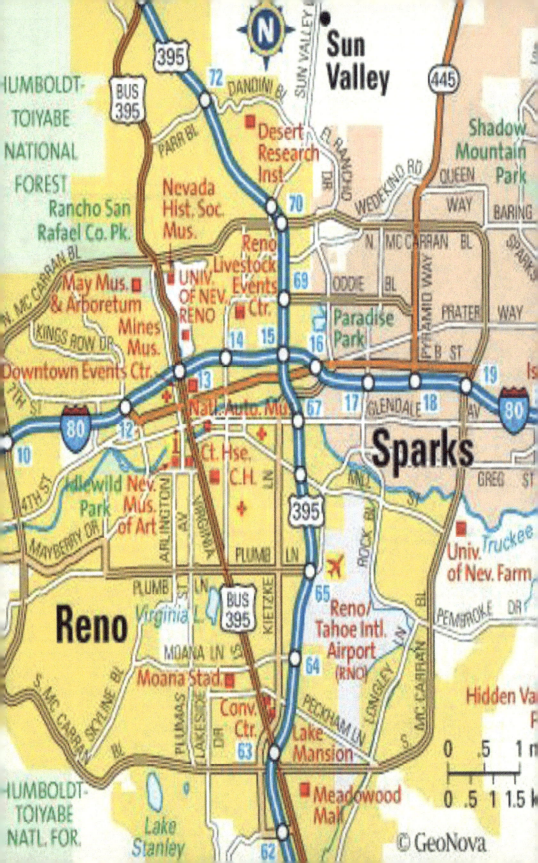

COPYRIGHT

Disclaimer

The information provided in this guide is intended for general reference purposes only. While every effort has been made to ensure accuracy and reliability, travel conditions, prices, and other details may change over time. Readers are advised to independently verify all information before making travel arrangements or decisions. The author and publisher of this guide disclaim any liability for damages, losses, or inconveniences that may arise from the use of the information presented herein. Travelers are encouraged to exercise caution, adhere to local laws and customs, and prioritize their safety at all times. Travelers are encouraged to conduct additional research and seek updated information from official sources.

BONUS(TRAVEL ESSENTIAL)

- Passport
- Flight Tickets
- Hotel Reservations
- Travel Insurance
- Credit Cards/Debit Cards
- Cash
- Travel Wallet
- Mobile Phone
- Chargers
- Portable Power Bank
- Headphones/Earphones
- Travel Adapter/Converter
- Luggage
- Daypack
- Packing Cubes
- Travel Locks
- Travel Pillow
- Sleep Mask
- Toiletries (Toothbrush, Toothpaste, Shampoo, etc.)
- First Aid Kit
- Prescription Medications
- Sunscreen
- Insect Repellent
- Sunglasses
- Hat
- Umbrella or Rain Jacket
- Travel Towel
- Swimsuit
- Flip-flops/Sandals
- Comfortable Walking Shoes
- Lightweight Clothing (Depending on Climate)

- o Travel Journal/Notebook
- o Pen
- o Travel Guidebook/Maps
- o Snacks
- o Water Bottle
- o Travel Mug
- o Camera/Smartphone
- o Copies of Important Documents (Passport, IDs, Itinerary

RENO TRAVEL GUIDE

Table of Contents

RENO TRAVEL GUIDE

RENO TRAVEL GUIDE

RENO TRAVEL GUIDE

Welcome to Reno: Your Gateway to Adventure!

Welcome, traveler, to the vibrant city of Reno! Nestled in the picturesque landscapes of the Sierra Nevada mountains, Reno beckons with its unique blend of outdoor adventures, cultural richness, and exhilarating entertainment.

As you embark on your journey through these pages, allow yourself to be swept away by the boundless opportunities that await you in the Biggest Little City in the World. Whether you're here to explore our scenic trails, indulge in culinary delights, or try your luck at the tables, Reno promises an unforgettable experience at every turn.

Within these chapters, you'll discover insider tips, hidden gems, and must-see attractions carefully curated to ensure that your time in Reno is nothing short of extraordinary. From the shimmering lights of our renowned casinos to the tranquil beauty of Lake Tahoe, there's something here for every adventurer, thrill-seeker, and culture enthusiast.

So, whether you're a first-time visitor or a seasoned traveler returning to rediscover the magic of Reno, I invite you to dive in, explore with an open heart, and let the spirit of adventure guide you. Let this travel guide be your companion as you uncover the wonders of Reno and create memories to last a lifetime.

Welcome to Reno—a city pulsating with energy, brimming with possibilities, and ready to enchant you at every turn. Your adventure starts here!

Chapter 1: Introduction

GETTING TO KNOW RENO

Reno, aptly nicknamed "The Biggest Little City in the World," is a vibrant and dynamic destination nestled in the heart of the Sierra Nevada mountains in western Nevada, United States. Known for its captivating blend of natural beauty, rich history, and vibrant culture, Reno offers travelers a myriad of experiences to discover and enjoy.

Geographical Location

Situated at an elevation of approximately 4,500 feet above sea level, Reno occupies a prime location along the Truckee River valley, just east of the majestic Lake Tahoe. Its geographical proximity to the Sierra Nevada mountain range provides a stunning backdrop of rugged peaks, alpine forests, and crystal-clear lakes, making it a haven for outdoor enthusiasts year-round.

Climate

Reno boasts a semi-arid climate characterized by hot summers and cold winters, with plenty of sunshine throughout the year. Summer temperatures typically range from the 80s to 90s Fahrenheit (around 27-35°C), while winter brings cooler temperatures with occasional snowfall, particularly in the surrounding mountains. Spring and fall offer mild and pleasant weather, making them ideal seasons to explore the city and its surrounding natural wonders.

Notable Features

One of Reno's most iconic features is its lively downtown area, home to an array of world-class casinos, restaurants, shops, and entertainment venues. The Reno Arch, adorned with neon lights and the city's slogan, "The Biggest Little City in the World," serves as a beloved symbol of Reno's vibrant spirit and bustling energy.

History and Culture

Reno's history dates back to the mid-19th century when it began as a modest trading post along the Truckee River. With the arrival of the railroad in the late 1800s, Reno flourished as a bustling transportation hub, connecting the eastern and western United States. The legalization of gambling in the early 20th century propelled Reno into the spotlight, earning it a reputation as a premier gaming destination and the "Divorce Capital of the World" due to its lenient divorce laws.

Today, Reno celebrates its rich heritage through its historic districts, museums, and cultural institutions. Visitors can explore the Nevada Museum of Art, delve into the city's mining history at the Comstock History Center, or stroll through the vibrant Midtown District, known for its eclectic mix of shops, galleries, and restaurants.

Significance as a Destination

As a travel destination, Reno offers a diverse range of experiences for visitors of all interests and ages. Whether it's trying your luck at the gaming tables, exploring the great outdoors, or immersing yourself in the city's vibrant cultural scene, Reno promises an unforgettable adventure. Its central location also makes it an ideal base for exploring nearby attractions such as Lake Tahoe, Virginia City, and the stunning landscapes of the Sierra Nevada mountains.

In summary, Reno's unique blend of natural beauty, rich history, and vibrant culture makes it a destination unlike any other. Whether you're seeking excitement and entertainment or tranquility and outdoor adventure, Reno invites you to discover the allure of "The Biggest Little City in the World.

Highlights of special events and attractions in Reno for 2024.

As 2024 unfolds, Reno, Nevada, prepares to dazzle visitors with an exciting lineup of special events and attractions. From cultural festivals to sporting spectacles, the Biggest Little City in the World promises an unforgettable year filled with entertainment, excitement, and adventure. In this overview, we'll delve into the highlights of what awaits travelers in Reno in 2024, showcasing the city's vibrant spirit and diverse offerings.

Reno Rodeo

One of the most anticipated events in Reno is the annual Reno Rodeo, a celebration of western heritage and cowboy culture. Held in June, the Reno Rodeo features thrilling rodeo competitions, including bull riding, barrel racing, and steer wrestling, attracting top riders and competitors from around the world. Beyond the arena, visitors can enjoy live music, carnival rides, and delicious western cuisine, making it a must-see event for rodeo enthusiasts and families alike.

Hot August Nights

Get ready to turn back the clock and relive the golden age of classic cars and rock 'n' roll at Hot August Nights. This iconic event, held in August, transforms Reno into a nostalgic paradise, with vintage car shows, live music performances, and retro-themed activities lining the streets. Whether you're a car aficionado or simply love the nostalgia of the 1950s and '60s, Hot August Nights offers an electrifying experience that's sure to delight visitors of all ages.

Artown Festival

For lovers of art, culture, and creativity, Reno's Artown Festival is a month-long celebration not to be missed. Throughout the month of July, Artown showcases a diverse array of visual and performing arts events, including concerts, dance performances, art exhibitions, and workshops. From world-renowned artists to emerging talents, Artown brings the community together to celebrate the transformative power of the arts and ignite the imagination of all who attend.

Great Reno Balloon Race

Experience the magic of hot air ballooning at the Great Reno Balloon Race, held annually in September. This beloved event attracts hundreds of colorful balloons and thousands of spectators to the skies above Reno for a weekend of breathtaking sights and family-friendly fun. Watch in awe as the sky fills with a dazzling array of balloons of all shapes and sizes, including special shapes like Darth Vader and the Energizer Bunny. With live music, food vendors, and a carnival atmosphere, the Great Reno Balloon Race is an enchanting spectacle that promises to lift spirits and create lasting memories for all who attend.

National Automobile Museum

Step back in time and explore the fascinating world of automotive history at the National Automobile Museum. Home to one of the most extensive collections of vintage and classic cars in the world, this museum offers a journey through the evolution of transportation, from the earliest horseless carriages to iconic sports cars and luxury automobiles. Highlights include the famous Harrah Collection, featuring rare and one-of-a-kind vehicles, as well as interactive exhibits and educational programs for visitors of all ages.

Truckee Riverwalk District

Take a leisurely stroll along the scenic Truckee Riverwalk District and discover the heart of downtown Reno. Lined with charming shops, galleries, restaurants, and cafes, this vibrant pedestrian-friendly area offers something for everyone. Enjoy waterfront dining with picturesque views of the river, browse local art galleries and boutiques, or simply relax in one of the many parks and public spaces along the riverbank. Whether you're looking for outdoor recreation, cultural experiences, or simply a place to unwind, the Truckee Riverwalk District is a hidden gem waiting to be explored.

Conclusion

In conclusion, Reno's lineup of special events and attractions for 2024 promises a year filled with excitement, entertainment, and adventure. Whether you're a fan of rodeo thrills, classic cars, artistic expression, or outdoor exploration, Reno offers something for every traveler to enjoy. So mark your calendars, pack your bags, and get ready to experience the best that the Biggest Little City in the World has to offer in 2024. From the heart-pounding action of the Reno Rodeo to the whimsical beauty of the Great Reno Balloon Race, Reno invites you to discover the magic and excitement that await around every corner.

Chapter 2: Getting There

Overview of Transportation Options in Reno

Reno, nestled in the heart of Nevada, offers a variety of transportation options to explore the city and its surrounding attractions. From public transportation to rental cars and bicycles, travelers have plenty of choices to navigate the area conveniently.

Public Transportation

Reno's public transportation system primarily consists of buses operated by the Regional Transportation Commission (RTC). The RTC offers several bus routes covering key areas within the city and neighboring communities. Riders can access route maps, schedules, and fare information on the RTC website or at designated transit centers. Passes and tickets can be purchased onboard buses or at RTC ticket outlets.

For effective use of public transportation, travelers are advised to familiarize themselves with route maps and schedules beforehand. Additionally, passengers should arrive at bus stops a few minutes early to ensure they don't miss their ride. When boarding the bus, it's essential to have the correct fare or pass ready, as drivers typically don't provide change.

Taxi and Ridesharing Services

Taxis are readily available in Reno, and they can be hailed from designated taxi stands or by calling a local cab company. Fares are usually metered, but it's a good practice to confirm the rate with the driver before starting the trip. Additionally, ridesharing services like Uber and Lyft operate in Reno, offering convenient and affordable transportation options. Travelers can download the respective apps, register for an account, and request rides from their smartphones. Safety tips include verifying the driver's identity and confirming the vehicle details before getting in.

Rental Cars and Driving

Renting a car is a popular choice for travelers who prefer flexibility and independence. Several car rental companies operate at Reno-Tahoe International Airport and throughout the city. Renters typically need a valid driver's license, a credit card, and must meet the minimum age requirement, which is usually 21 years old. It's essential to familiarize yourself with local driving regulations, including speed limits, traffic signs, and parking rules. While driving in Reno is generally straightforward, travelers should be mindful of potential congestion, especially during peak hours.

Bicycles and Walking

Exploring Reno by bike or on foot offers a unique perspective and allows travelers to immerse themselves in the city's charm. Several bike rental shops offer daily or hourly rentals, allowing visitors to pedal along designated bike lanes and scenic trails. Pedestrian-friendly areas like the

Truckee Riverwalk District and downtown Reno are perfect for leisurely strolls and self-guided walking tours. Safety tips for cyclists include wearing helmets, obeying traffic laws, and using hand signals when turning.

Navigating Landmarks and Points of Interest

Travelers can reach popular landmarks and attractions in Reno using various transportation modes. Buses and ridesharing services provide convenient access to downtown casinos, museums, and entertainment venues. Rental cars offer flexibility for exploring farther afield, including nearby attractions like Lake Tahoe and Virginia City. For pedestrians, many landmarks are within walking distance of downtown hotels, making it easy to explore on foot.

Accessibility Information

Reno strives to provide accessible transportation options for travelers with disabilities. RTC buses are equipped with wheelchair ramps and priority seating, and service animals are welcome onboard. Travelers requiring additional assistance can contact RTC's customer service for personalized support and information on accessible routes and facilities.

Safety and Security Tips

When using transportation services in Reno, travelers should prioritize safety and security. Avoiding unlicensed taxis and ridesharing vehicles, especially late at night, can help prevent potential scams or safety concerns. It's advisable to keep belongings secure and be vigilant, especially in crowded areas or tourist hotspots. In case of emergencies, travelers should know how to contact local authorities or seek assistance from nearby businesses or residents.

Local Etiquette and Customs

Respecting local customs and etiquette is essential when using transportation in Reno. Tipping is customary for taxi drivers and rideshare drivers, with 15-20% of the fare being a typical gratuity. Queueing politely and allowing passengers to disembark before boarding buses or trains demonstrates courtesy and respect for fellow travelers. Additionally, maintaining a friendly and respectful demeanor towards drivers and fellow passengers contributes to a positive transportation experience for everyone.

Additional Resources

For further information on transportation in Reno, travelers can consult helpful resources such as the RTC website, which provides schedules, maps, and contact information for customer service. Mobile apps like Transit and Google Maps offer real-time transit information and trip planning tools, making it easier to navigate the city. Tourist information centers and hotel concierge services can also provide assistance with transportation inquiries and recommendations for getting around Reno efficiently. In case of emergencies or urgent assistance, travelers can save contact details for local transportation authorities, tourist information centers, and emergency services for quick access when needed.

Nearest airports and their distances from Reno.

Reno, Nevada, is served by Reno-Tahoe International Airport (RNO), located approximately 3 miles southeast of downtown Reno. Reno-Tahoe International Airport is the primary commercial airport serving the Reno-Sparks metropolitan area and offers a range of domestic and international flights.

For travelers seeking alternative airport options, the closest major airport to Reno is Sacramento International Airport (SMF), located approximately 135 miles southwest of Reno in Sacramento, California. Sacramento International Airport offers a wider selection of flights and airlines compared to Reno-Tahoe International Airport, making it a viable option for travelers willing to drive a bit farther for more convenient flight options.

Additionally, travelers may consider using San Francisco International Airport (SFO), located approximately 220 miles southwest of Reno in San Francisco, California. While SFO is further away than Sacramento International Airport, it offers even more extensive flight options, including numerous international destinations, making it a suitable choice for travelers seeking a wider range of flight connections.

In summary, Reno-Tahoe International Airport is the nearest airport to Reno, offering convenient access to the city and surrounding areas. However, travelers looking for a broader selection of flights may consider Sacramento International Airport or San Francisco International Airport as alternative options, depending on their travel preferences and itinerary.

Visa and Traveling Documents Needed to Enter Reno

Before embarking on your journey to Reno, Nevada, it's essential to ensure you have the necessary visa and traveling documents to enter the United States. Whether you're visiting for leisure, business, or other purposes, understanding the visa requirements and documentation process is crucial for a smooth and hassle-free travel experience.

Visa Requirements for Entry into the United States

The visa requirements for entering the United States vary depending on your country of citizenship and the purpose of your visit. Citizens of countries participating in the Visa Waiver Program (VWP) may be eligible to travel to the United States for tourism or business purposes without obtaining a visa. However, they must apply for an Electronic System for Travel Authorization (ESTA) online before traveling.

For citizens of countries not eligible for the VWP, obtaining a nonimmigrant visa from a U.S. embassy or consulate is typically required for entry into the United States. The specific visa category will depend on the purpose of your visit, such as tourism, business, study, or work.

Entering Reno via Reno-Tahoe International Airport

Reno-Tahoe International Airport serves as the primary gateway for travelers arriving in Reno by air. Upon arrival, all international passengers must proceed through U.S. Customs and Border Protection (CBP) clearance, regardless of their visa status. CBP officers will verify travelers' documents, including passports, visas, and ESTA approvals, if applicable, and may conduct interviews to determine the purpose of the visit and ensure compliance with immigration laws.

Documentation Required for Entry into the United States

To enter the United States, travelers must possess the following essential documents:

1. **Passport**: A valid passport is required for all international travelers entering the United

States. The passport must be valid for at least six months beyond the intended period of stay in the U.S.

2. **Visa or ESTA**: Depending on your country of citizenship and the purpose of your visit, you may need a nonimmigrant visa or an approved ESTA. Ensure that your visa or ESTA is valid for the duration of your intended stay in the United States.

3. **Return or Onward Ticket**: CBP officers may request proof of a return or onward ticket to ensure that travelers do not intend to stay in the United States beyond the authorized period.

4. **Proof of Sufficient Funds**: Travelers may be asked to provide evidence of sufficient funds to cover their expenses during their stay in the United States, including accommodation, meals, and transportation.

5. **Customs Declaration Form**: All travelers must complete a Customs Declaration Form (CBP Form 6059B) before arrival, declaring any items they are bringing into the United States, including currency, gifts, and merchandise.

Tips for Smooth Entry into the United States

To facilitate a smooth entry into the United States, consider the following tips:

- Ensure that all travel documents, including passports, visas, and ESTA approvals, are up to date and valid for the duration of your stay in the United States.
- Familiarize yourself with U.S. immigration laws and regulations to understand your rights and responsibilities as a visitor.
- Arrive at the airport well in advance of your scheduled departure to allow ample time for check-in, security screening, and immigration clearance.
- Be prepared to answer questions from CBP officers truthfully and confidently, providing clear and concise responses regarding the purpose of your visit and your intended activities in the United States.
- Respect all customs and immigration procedures, follow instructions from CBP officers, and remain patient and cooperative throughout the entry process.

Conclusion

In conclusion, ensuring you have the necessary visa and traveling documents is essential for a successful trip to Reno, Nevada, and the United States. By understanding the visa requirements, obtaining the appropriate documentation, and adhering to customs and immigration procedures, you can enjoy a smooth and hassle-free entry into the country. Whether you're visiting for leisure, business, or other purposes, proper preparation and compliance with immigration laws will help make your journey to Reno a memorable and enjoyable experience.

Best Time to Visit Reno

Reno, known as "The Biggest Little City in the World," offers a diverse range of attractions and activities throughout the year. When planning your visit to Reno, consider the weather, seasons, and local events to make the most of your trip.

1. Spring (March to May):

- Spring in Reno brings mild temperatures and blooming landscapes, making it an ideal time for outdoor activities such as hiking, biking, and exploring the city.
- The Reno River Festival, held in May, attracts outdoor enthusiasts and features kayaking competitions, live music, and food vendors along the Truckee River.

2. Summer (June to August):

- Summer in Reno brings warm temperatures, perfect for enjoying outdoor festivals, concerts, and water activities on the Truckee River or nearby Lake Tahoe.
- The Artown festival in July showcases a variety of cultural events, including live music, art exhibits, and performances throughout the city.

3. Fall (September to November):

- Fall is a delightful time to visit Reno, with pleasant weather and vibrant fall foliage in the surrounding Sierra Nevada mountains.
- The Great Reno Balloon Race in September is a popular event, where colorful hot air balloons fill the sky for a spectacular sight.

4. Winter (December to February):

- Winter transforms Reno into a winter wonderland, offering opportunities for skiing, snowboarding, and other snow sports in nearby Lake Tahoe resorts.
- The Reno Santa Pub Crawl in December is a festive event where participants dress up as

Santa Claus and visit various bars and pubs throughout the city.

5. Year-Round Events:

- Reno hosts several year-round events and attractions, including casino gaming, live entertainment, and cultural festivals.
- The National Automobile Museum, Reno Arch, and Nevada Museum of Art are popular attractions worth visiting regardless of the season.

Overall, the best time to visit Reno depends on your preferences and interests. Whether you're seeking outdoor adventures, cultural experiences, or vibrant nightlife, Reno has something to offer year-round. Be sure to check local event calendars and weather forecasts when planning your trip to make the most of your visit to this dynamic city.

Chapter 3: Accommodation

Recommended Budget-Friendly Accommodations in Reno

1. Sands Regency Casino Hotel

- **Price Range:** $50 - $100 per night
- **Features and Amenities:** Casino, outdoor pool, fitness center, multiple dining options, free Wi-Fi.

- **Booking Platforms:** Booking.com, Expedia, Hotels.com
- **Local Regulations and Customs:** Check-in after 3:00 PM, check-out before 11:00 AM. Tipping practices are customary, with 15-20% gratuity expected.
- **Special Features:** Suitable for solo travelers and couples. Accessible rooms available for guests with disabilities.
- **Transportation:** Shuttle service to Reno-Tahoe International Airport. Public transportation stops nearby.

2. Circus Circus Reno

- **Price Range:** $60 - $120 per night
- **Features and Amenities:** On-site casino, circus performances, arcade, family-friendly activities, multiple dining options.
- **Booking Platforms:** Booking.com, Expedia, Priceline
- **Local Regulations and Customs:** Check-in after 4:00 PM, check-out before 11:00 AM. Tipping is customary.
- **Special Features:** Ideal for families with children. Pet-friendly accommodations and wheelchair-accessible rooms available.

- **Transportation:** Complimentary shuttle service to Reno-Tahoe International Airport. Easy access to public transportation.

3. Eldorado Resort Casino

- **Price Range:** $70 - $150 per night
- **Features and Amenities:** Casino, fitness center, outdoor pool, spa, multiple dining options.
- **Booking Platforms:** Hotels.com, Expedia, Orbitz
- **Local Regulations and Customs:** Check-in after 3:00 PM, check-out before 12:00 PM. Tipping is customary.
- **Special Features:** Suitable for couples and solo travelers. Accessible rooms available upon request.
- **Transportation:** Shuttle service to/from Reno-Tahoe International Airport. Easy access to public transportation.

4. Motel 6 Reno - Livestock Events Center

- **Price Range:** $40 - $80 per night
- **Features and Amenities:** Pet-friendly accommodation, outdoor pool, free parking, Wi-Fi available.

- **Booking Platforms:** Motel6.com, Booking.com, Expedia
- **Local Regulations and Customs:** Check-in after 3:00 PM, check-out before 11:00 AM. Tipping is appreciated but not mandatory.
- **Special Features:** Ideal for budget-conscious travelers and pet owners. Accessible rooms available upon request.
- **Transportation:** Close to major highways and public transport routes. Taxi services available.

5. Baymont by Wyndham Reno

- **Price Range:** $50 - $100 per night
- **Features and Amenities:** Complimentary breakfast, outdoor pool, fitness center, free parking, Wi-Fi available.
- **Booking Platforms:** WyndhamHotels.com, Booking.com, Expedia
- **Local Regulations and Customs:** Check-in after 3:00 PM, check-out before 11:00 AM. Tipping is customary.
- **Special Features:** Suitable for families and solo travelers. Accessible rooms available upon request.

- **Transportation:** Shuttle service to Reno-Tahoe International Airport. Easy access to public transportation.

6. Quality Inn & Suites Reno

- **Price Range:** $50 - $100 per night
- **Features and Amenities:** Complimentary breakfast, outdoor pool, fitness center, free parking, Wi-Fi available.
- **Booking Platforms:** ChoiceHotels.com, Booking.com, Expedia
- **Local Regulations and Customs:** Check-in after 3:00 PM, check-out before 11:00 AM. Tipping is customary.
- **Special Features:** Ideal for families and solo travelers. Accessible rooms available upon request.
- **Transportation:** Close to major highways. Taxi services available. Public transportation nearby.

7. Super 8 by Wyndham Meadow Wood Courtyard

- **Price Range:** $50 - $100 per night

- **Features and Amenities:** Complimentary breakfast, outdoor pool, free parking, Wi-Fi available.
- **Booking Platforms:** WyndhamHotels.com, Booking.com, Expedia
- **Local Regulations and Customs:** Check-in after 3:00 PM, check-out before 11:00 AM. Tipping is customary.
- **Special Features:** Ideal for budget-conscious travelers. Accessible rooms available upon request.
- **Transportation:** Close to major highways. Taxi services available. Public transportation stops nearby.

8. Legacy Vacation Resorts - Reno

- **Price Range:** $60 - $120 per night
- **Features and Amenities:** Studio and suite accommodations, kitchenette, outdoor pool, hot tub, fitness center, Wi-Fi available.
- **Booking Platforms:** Booking.com, Expedia, Hotels.com
- **Local Regulations and Customs:** Check-in after 4:00 PM, check-out before 10:00 AM. Tipping is customary.

- **Special Features:** Ideal for families and extended stays. Accessible accommodations available upon request.
- **Transportation:** Shuttle service to downtown Reno and nearby attractions. Close to public transportation routes.

9. Plaza Resort Club

- **Price Range:** $70 - $150 per night
- **Features and Amenities:** Studio and suite accommodations, kitchenette, fitness center, indoor pool, hot tub, free Wi-Fi.
- **Booking Platforms:** Booking.com, Expedia, Hotels.com
- **Local Regulations and Customs:** Check-in after 4:00 PM, check-out before 11:00 AM. Tipping is customary.
- **Special Features:** Suitable for families and extended stays. Accessible accommodations available upon request.
- **Transportation:** Shuttle service to downtown Reno and nearby attractions. Close to public transportation routes.

10. Siegel Suites Reno Sparks

- **Price Range:** $40 - $80 per night

- **Features and Amenities:** Studio and suite accommodations, kitchenette, free parking, Wi-Fi available.
- **Booking Platforms:** Booking.com, Expedia, SiegelSuites.com
- **Local Regulations and Customs:** Check-in after 3:00 PM, check-out before 11:00 AM. Tipping is appreciated but not mandatory.
- **Special Features:** Ideal for long-term stays. Accessible accommodations available upon request.
- **Transportation:** Close to public transportation routes. Taxi services available. Easy access to major highways.

Mid-Range Accommodations in Reno

1. Whitney Peak Hotel

- **Price Range:** $100 - $200 per night
- **Features and Amenities:** Boutique hotel, on-site restaurant, outdoor climbing wall, fitness center, pet-friendly rooms, complimentary Wi-Fi.
- **Booking Platforms:** Booking.com, Expedia, Hotels.com
- **Local Regulations and Customs:** Check-in after 4:00 PM, check-out before 11:00 AM. Tipping is customary for hotel services.
- **Special Features:** Ideal for solo travelers and outdoor enthusiasts. Accessible rooms available. Highly recommended by locals for its central location and unique amenities.
- **Transportation:** Shuttle service available. Close to public transportation stops.

2. Renaissance Reno Downtown Hotel

- **Price Range:** $150 - $250 per night
- **Features and Amenities:** Modern hotel, rooftop pool and bar, fitness center, on-site

dining, business center, complimentary Wi-Fi.

- **Booking Platforms:** Marriott.com, Booking.com, Expedia
- **Local Regulations and Customs:** Check-in after 3:00 PM, check-out before 12:00 PM. Tipping is customary.
- **Special Features:** Suitable for business travelers and couples. Accessible rooms available. Guests praise the rooftop pool and convenient downtown location.
- **Transportation:** Close to public transportation options. Taxi services readily available.

3. Hyatt Place Reno-Tahoe Airport

- **Price Range:** $120 - $200 per night
- **Features and Amenities:** Airport hotel, complimentary breakfast, outdoor pool, 24/7 fitness center, pet-friendly rooms, free Wi-Fi.
- **Booking Platforms:** Hyatt.com, Booking.com, Expedia
- **Local Regulations and Customs:** Check-in after 3:00 PM, check-out before 12:00 PM. Tipping is customary.

- **Special Features:** Convenient for travelers flying in and out of Reno-Tahoe International Airport. Accessible accommodations available. Recommended for families and pet owners.
- **Transportation:** Complimentary airport shuttle service. Easy access to major highways.

4. Silver Legacy Resort Casino

- **Price Range:** $120 - $220 per night
- **Features and Amenities:** Casino resort, multiple dining options, outdoor pool, spa, entertainment venue, free Wi-Fi.
- **Booking Platforms:** Booking.com, Expedia, Hotels.com
- **Local Regulations and Customs:** Check-in after 3:00 PM, check-out before 12:00 PM. Tipping is customary.
- **Special Features:** Ideal for couples and families. Wheelchair-accessible rooms available. Guests appreciate the variety of dining and entertainment options.
- **Transportation:** Shuttle service to and from the airport. Close to public transportation stops.

5. Courtyard by Marriott Reno Downtown/Riverfront

- **Price Range:** $130 - $220 per night
- **Features and Amenities:** Riverfront hotel, outdoor terrace, fitness center, on-site dining, business center, free Wi-Fi.
- **Booking Platforms:** Marriott.com, Booking.com, Expedia
- **Local Regulations and Customs:** Check-in after 3:00 PM, check-out before 12:00 PM. Tipping is customary.
- **Special Features:** Great for business travelers and couples. Accessible accommodations available. Guests praise the scenic river views and convenient location.
- **Transportation:** Close to public transportation options. Taxi services readily available.

6. Grand Sierra Resort and Casino

- **Price Range:** $100 - $200 per night
- **Features and Amenities:** Casino resort, multiple dining options, outdoor pool, spa, entertainment venue, golf course, free Wi-Fi.

- **Booking Platforms:** Booking.com, Expedia, Hotels.com
- **Local Regulations and Customs:** Check-in after 3:00 PM, check-out before 12:00 PM. Tipping is customary.
- **Special Features:** Suitable for families and couples. Accessible rooms available. Highly recommended for its variety of amenities and entertainment options.
- **Transportation:** Shuttle service to and from the airport. Close to public transportation stops.

7. Homewood Suites by Hilton Reno

- **Price Range:** $140 - $230 per night
- **Features and Amenities:** All-suite hotel, complimentary breakfast, evening socials, outdoor pool, fitness center, pet-friendly rooms, free Wi-Fi.
- **Booking Platforms:** Hilton.com, Booking.com, Expedia
- **Local Regulations and Customs:** Check-in after 3:00 PM, check-out before 12:00 PM. Tipping is customary.
- **Special Features:** Ideal for families and extended stays. Accessible accommodations

available. Guests appreciate the spacious suites and complimentary amenities.

- **Transportation:** Close to public transportation options. Taxi services readily available.

8. Holiday Inn Express & Suites Reno

- **Price Range:** $110 - $180 per night
- **Features and Amenities:** Complimentary breakfast, indoor pool, fitness center, business center, free Wi-Fi.
- **Booking Platforms:** IHG.com, Booking.com, Expedia
- **Local Regulations and Customs:** Check-in after 3:00 PM, check-out before 12:00 PM. Tipping is customary.
- **Special Features:** Suitable for families and business travelers. Accessible accommodations available. Guests praise the clean rooms and convenient amenities.
- **Transportation:** Close to public transportation options. Taxi services readily available.

9. Hampton Inn & Suites Reno West

- **Price Range:** $120 - $200 per night

- **Features and Amenities:** Complimentary breakfast, indoor pool, fitness center, business center, free Wi-Fi.
- **Booking Platforms:** Hilton.com, Booking.com, Expedia
- **Local Regulations and Customs:** Check-in after 3:00 PM, check-out before 12:00 PM. Tipping is customary.
- **Special Features:** Suitable for families and business travelers. Accessible accommodations available. Guests appreciate the friendly staff and comfortable rooms.
- **Transportation:** Close to public transportation options. Taxi services readily available.

10. SpringHill Suites by Marriott Reno

- **Price Range:** $130 - $220 per night
- **Features and Amenities:** All-suite hotel, complimentary breakfast, outdoor pool, fitness center, business center, free Wi-Fi.
- **Booking Platforms:** Marriott.com, Booking.com, Expedia
- **Local Regulations and Customs:** Check-in after 3:00 PM, check-out before 12:00 PM. Tipping is customary.

- **Special Features:** Suitable for families and business travelers. Accessible accommodations available. Guests praise the spacious suites and convenient amenities.
- **Transportation:** Close to public transportation options. Taxi services readily available.

Luxury Accommodations in Reno

1. Peppermill Resort Spa Casino

- **Price Range:** $200 - $400 per night
- **Features and Amenities:** Luxurious rooms, spa, multiple pools, fine dining restaurants, casino, nightclub, entertainment venue.
- **Booking Platforms:** Booking.com, Expedia, Hotels.com
- **Local Regulations and Customs:** Check-in after 3:00 PM, check-out before 12:00 PM. Tipping is customary for hotel services.
- **Special Features:** Ideal for couples and luxury travelers. Accessible rooms available. Guests praise the upscale ambiance and variety of amenities.

- **Transportation:** Shuttle service to and from the airport. Close to public transportation stops.

2. Atlantis Casino Resort Spa

- **Price Range:** $250 - $500 per night
- **Features and Amenities:** Elegant rooms, spa, indoor and outdoor pools, multiple dining options, casino, entertainment venue.
- **Booking Platforms:** Booking.com, Expedia, Hotels.com
- **Local Regulations and Customs:** Check-in after 4:00 PM, check-out before 11:00 AM. Tipping is customary.
- **Special Features:** Suitable for couples and luxury travelers. Accessible rooms available. Guests appreciate the upscale accommodations and attentive service.
- **Transportation:** Shuttle service to and from the airport. Close to public transportation stops.

3. Grand Sierra Resort and Casino

- **Price Range:** $200 - $400 per night

- **Features and Amenities:** Luxury rooms, spa, outdoor pool, golf course, multiple dining options, entertainment venue, casino.
- **Booking Platforms:** Booking.com, Expedia, Hotels.com
- **Local Regulations and Customs:** Check-in after 3:00 PM, check-out before 12:00 PM. Tipping is customary.
- **Special Features:** Ideal for families and luxury travelers. Accessible rooms available. Guests praise the expansive property and upscale amenities.
- **Transportation:** Shuttle service to and from the airport. Close to public transportation stops.

4. Silver Legacy Resort Casino

- **Price Range:** $200 - $400 per night
- **Features and Amenities:** Sophisticated rooms, spa, outdoor pool, multiple dining options, entertainment venue, casino.
- **Booking Platforms:** Booking.com, Expedia, Hotels.com
- **Local Regulations and Customs:** Check-in after 3:00 PM, check-out before 12:00 PM. Tipping is customary.

- **Special Features:** Suitable for couples and luxury travelers. Accessible rooms available. Guests appreciate the upscale accommodations and variety of entertainment options.
- **Transportation:** Shuttle service to and from the airport. Close to public transportation stops.

5. Whitney Peak Hotel

- **Price Range:** $250 - $500 per night
- **Features and Amenities:** Boutique luxury hotel, upscale rooms, rooftop bar, fitness center, pet-friendly accommodations, complimentary Wi-Fi.
- **Booking Platforms:** Booking.com, Expedia, Hotels.com
- **Local Regulations and Customs:** Check-in after 4:00 PM, check-out before 11:00 AM. Tipping is customary for hotel services.
- **Special Features:** Ideal for couples and luxury travelers. Accessible rooms available. Guests praise the modern ambiance and excellent service.
- **Transportation:** Shuttle service available. Close to public transportation stops.

6. Renaissance Reno Downtown Hotel

- **Price Range:** $300 - $600 per night
- **Features and Amenities:** Upscale rooms, rooftop pool and bar, fitness center, on-site dining, business center, free Wi-Fi.
- **Booking Platforms:** Marriott.com, Booking.com, Expedia
- **Local Regulations and Customs:** Check-in after 3:00 PM, check-out before 12:00 PM. Tipping is customary.
- **Special Features:** Suitable for couples and luxury travelers. Accessible rooms available. Guests praise the modern design and convenient downtown location.
- **Transportation:** Close to public transportation options. Taxi services readily available.

7. The Row at Eldorado, Silver Legacy, Circus Circus

- **Price Range:** $250 - $500 per night
- **Features and Amenities:** Luxurious rooms, spa, outdoor pool, multiple dining options, entertainment venues, casino.
- **Booking Platforms:** Booking.com, Expedia, Hotels.com

- **Local Regulations and Customs:** Check-in after 3:00 PM, check-out before 12:00 PM. Tipping is customary.
- **Special Features:** Ideal for couples and luxury travelers. Accessible rooms available. Guests appreciate the variety of dining and entertainment options.
- **Transportation:** Shuttle service to and from the airport. Close to public transportation stops.

8. Hyatt Regency Lake Tahoe Resort, Spa and Casino

- **Price Range:** $300 - $600 per night
- **Features and Amenities:** Lakeside luxury resort, spa, outdoor pool, multiple dining options, casino.
- **Booking Platforms:** Hyatt.com, Booking.com, Expedia
- **Local Regulations and Customs:** Check-in after 4:00 PM, check-out before 11:00 AM. Tipping is customary.
- **Special Features:** Ideal for couples and luxury travelers. Accessible rooms available. Guests praise the serene lakeside setting and upscale amenities.

- **Transportation:** Shuttle service to and from the airport. Close to public transportation stops.

9. The Ritz-Carlton Lake Tahoe

- **Price Range:** $500 - $1000 per night
- **Features and Amenities:** Luxury mountain resort, spa, outdoor pool, fine dining restaurant, ski-in/ski-out access.
- **Booking Platforms:** Marriott.com, Booking.com, Expedia
- **Local Regulations and Customs:** Check-in after 4:00 PM, check-out before 12:00 PM. Tipping is customary.
- **Special Features:** Ideal for couples and luxury travelers. Accessible rooms available. Guests praise the impeccable service and scenic mountain views.
- **Transportation:** Shuttle service to and from the airport. Close to public transportation stops.

10. Resort at Squaw Creek

- **Price Range:** $400 - $800 per night

- **Features and Amenities:** Luxury mountain resort, spa, outdoor pool, multiple dining options, golf course, ski-in/ski-out access.
- **Booking Platforms:** Booking.com, Expedia, Hotels.com
- **Local Regulations and Customs:** Check-in after 4:00 PM, check-out before 11:00 AM. Tipping is customary.
- **Special Features:** Ideal for couples and luxury travelers. Accessible rooms available. Guests appreciate the stunning mountain setting and array of outdoor activities.
- **Transportation:** Shuttle service to and from the airport. Close to public transportation stops.

Unconventional Accommodation Options in Reno

Reno, known for its vibrant entertainment and outdoor adventures, also offers a range of unique and unconventional accommodation options for travelers seeking something different. From boutique hotels and eco-lodges to cozy homestays and rustic farm stays, there's a variety of offbeat places to stay in Reno. Here are five unconventional accommodations worth considering:

1. The Jesse Hotel & Bar

- **Price Range:** $100 - $200 per night
- **Features and Amenities:** Stylish boutique hotel with modern decor, rooftop bar, complimentary breakfast, bicycle rentals.
- **Booking Platforms:** Booking.com, Expedia, Hotels.com
- **Local Regulations and Customs:** Check-in after 3:00 PM, check-out before 11:00 AM. Tipping is customary for hotel services.
- **Special Features:** Ideal for solo travelers and couples. Pet-friendly rooms available upon request. Guests appreciate the trendy design and convenient downtown location.

- **Transportation:** Close to public transportation stops. Taxi services readily available.

2. The Depot Craft Brewery Distillery

- **Price Range:** $150 - $300 per night
- **Features and Amenities:** Unique accommodation located above a craft brewery and distillery, tasting room, farm-to-table restaurant.
- **Booking Platforms:** Airbnb, Booking.com, Expedia
- **Local Regulations and Customs:** Check-in after 4:00 PM, check-out before 11:00 AM. Tipping is customary for restaurant and bar services.
- **Special Features:** Best suited for couples and foodies. Not recommended for families with young children due to the onsite brewery. Guests praise the cozy atmosphere and delicious craft beverages.
- **Transportation:** Close to public transportation stops. Taxi services readily available.

3. Sierra Safari Zoo Guest Cottages

- **Price Range:** $80 - $150 per night
- **Features and Amenities:** Quaint cottages located within a wildlife sanctuary, access to the zoo, picnic areas.
- **Booking Platforms:** Airbnb, Booking.com, Expedia
- **Local Regulations and Customs:** Check-in after 3:00 PM, check-out before 12:00 PM. Tipping is appreciated for zoo staff.
- **Special Features:** Ideal for families and animal lovers. Accessible cottages available. Guests enjoy the unique experience of staying overnight in a zoo and interacting with the animals.
- **Transportation:** Close to public transportation stops. Taxi services readily available.

4. River Inn at Truckee River

- **Price Range:** $120 - $250 per night
- **Features and Amenities:** Charming riverside inn with cozy rooms, riverside patio, complimentary breakfast, bike rentals.
- **Booking Platforms:** Booking.com, Expedia, Hotels.com

- **Local Regulations and Customs:** Check-in after 3:00 PM, check-out before 11:00 AM. Tipping is customary for hotel services.
- **Special Features:** Suitable for couples and outdoor enthusiasts. Pet-friendly rooms available upon request. Guests love the tranquil riverside setting and proximity to outdoor activities.
- **Transportation:** Close to public transportation stops. Taxi services readily available.

5. Rancho San Rafael Park Homestay

- **Price Range:** $50 - $100 per night
- **Features and Amenities:** Cozy guest room in a private home, access to Rancho San Rafael Park, continental breakfast.
- **Booking Platforms:** Airbnb, Booking.com, Expedia
- **Local Regulations and Customs:** Check-in and check-out times flexible, depending on host availability. Tipping is not expected but appreciated for hospitality.
- **Special Features:** Ideal for solo travelers and budget-conscious visitors. Accessible room available upon request. Guests

appreciate the warm hospitality and proximity to nature trails.

- **Transportation:** Close to public transportation stops. Taxi services readily available.

In conclusion, Reno offers a range of unique and unconventional accommodation options for travelers looking for a memorable stay. Whether you prefer a trendy boutique hotel, a rustic farm stay, or a cozy homestay, there's something for everyone to enjoy in "The Biggest Little City in the World." Be sure to book in advance and consider your preferences and budget when choosing the perfect accommodation for your Reno adventure!

Chapter 4: Things to Do

Overview of must-see attractions in Reno.

Reno, Nevada, often referred to as "The Biggest Little City in the World," is a vibrant destination filled with an array of attractions that cater to every interest and age group. From outdoor adventures to cultural experiences and lively entertainment options, Reno offers something for everyone. Here is an overview of the must-see attractions that should be on your itinerary when visiting Reno.

1. The National Automobile Museum:

- The National Automobile Museum, also known as the Harrah Collection, is a must-visit attraction for automobile enthusiasts. This world-class museum houses over 200 vintage automobiles spanning more than a century of automotive history. Visitors can admire rare and iconic vehicles, including classic cars, celebrity-owned automobiles, and one-of-a-kind prototypes.

2. The Reno Riverwalk District:

- The Reno Riverwalk District is a scenic area along the Truckee River, offering a vibrant mix of shops, restaurants, art galleries, and entertainment venues. Visitors can stroll along the picturesque riverfront promenade, dine at waterfront restaurants, and enjoy live music and street performances. The Riverwalk also hosts seasonal events, such as the Reno River Festival and Artown, adding to its appeal as a cultural hub in the heart of downtown Reno.

3. The Nevada Museum of Art:

- The Nevada Museum of Art is the only accredited art museum in the state and is renowned for its diverse collection of contemporary and historical artworks. The museum's permanent collection features works by renowned artists such as Georgia O'Keeffe, Robert Beckmann, and Hans Meyer-Kassel. In addition to its exhibitions, the museum offers educational programs, lectures, and community events that engage visitors of all ages.

4. Lake Tahoe:

- Just a short drive from Reno, Lake Tahoe is a breathtaking natural wonder that attracts visitors year-round. Surrounded by the majestic Sierra Nevada mountains, Lake Tahoe offers pristine beaches, crystal-clear waters, and a wealth of outdoor recreational activities. Visitors can enjoy swimming, boating, fishing, hiking, and skiing, depending on the season. Whether you're seeking adventure or relaxation, Lake Tahoe is a must-see destination near Reno.

5. The Great Reno Balloon Race:

- The Great Reno Balloon Race is one of the largest hot air balloon festivals in the world and a beloved annual event in Reno. Held every September, the event attracts balloonists from around the globe who come to participate in colorful balloon races and dazzling night glow events. Spectators can marvel at the sight of hundreds of balloons filling the sky, creating a magical and unforgettable experience for all who attend.

6. Virginia City:

- Step back in time and experience the Wild West charm of Virginia City, located just a short drive from Reno. This historic mining town is known for its well-preserved 19th-century architecture, including saloons, museums, and old-fashioned storefronts. Visitors can take a ride on the historic Virginia & Truckee Railroad, explore underground mines, or simply soak in the atmosphere of this iconic Old West town.

7. The Reno Arch:

- The iconic Reno Arch is a symbol of the city's vibrant culture and history. Originally erected in 1926, the arch has undergone several renovations and upgrades over the years and remains a beloved landmark in downtown Reno. Visitors can snap photos beneath the illuminated arch, which welcomes guests to "The Biggest Little City in the World" in bold neon letters, creating a memorable backdrop for any visit to Reno.

8. Animal Ark:

- Animal Ark is a unique wildlife sanctuary located just outside of Reno, dedicated to the rescue and rehabilitation of injured and orphaned animals. The sanctuary is home to a diverse array of native and exotic species, including wolves, bears, cheetahs, and birds of prey. Visitors can take guided tours of the sanctuary, observe the animals in their natural habitats, and learn about conservation efforts to protect endangered species.

9. Wilbur D. May Center:

- The Wilbur D. May Center is a cultural and educational institution located in Rancho San Rafael Regional Park, offering a range of attractions for visitors of all ages. The center includes the Wilbur D. May Museum, featuring exhibits on natural history, anthropology, and world cultures, as well as the Arboretum and Botanical Garden, showcasing a diverse collection of plants and flowers. Visitors can also explore the May Arboretum Society's themed gardens, participate in educational programs, and enjoy outdoor recreational activities in the surrounding park.

10. The Sparks Marina:

- The Sparks Marina is a picturesque recreational area located in nearby Sparks, offering a tranquil escape from the hustle and bustle of city life. The marina features a sparkling 77-acre lake surrounded by sandy beaches, walking trails, and picnic areas. Visitors can enjoy swimming, kayaking, paddle boarding, and fishing, as well as scenic views of the surrounding mountains. The Sparks Marina is a popular destination for outdoor enthusiasts and families seeking leisurely activities in a beautiful natural setting.

Outdoor activities for nature lovers and adventure seekers.

Reno, nestled in the picturesque Sierra Nevada mountains, offers an abundance of outdoor activities for nature lovers and adventure seekers alike. From scenic hikes and thrilling water sports to adrenaline-pumping adventures, there's no shortage of opportunities to explore the natural beauty of the region. Here are some must-try outdoor activities to add to your itinerary when visiting Reno.

1. Hiking:

- Reno is surrounded by an extensive network of hiking trails that cater to hikers of all skill levels. Whether you're seeking a leisurely stroll through scenic meadows or a challenging ascent to panoramic viewpoints, there's a trail for you. Popular hiking destinations near Reno include the Mount Rose Trail, Hunter Creek Trail, and Tahoe Rim Trail, offering stunning vistas of the surrounding mountains, forests, and lakes.

2. Mountain Biking:

- With its rugged terrain and diverse landscapes, Reno is a paradise for mountain biking enthusiasts. The area boasts numerous mountain biking trails ranging from beginner-friendly paths to technical single tracks and downhill courses. Riders can explore the trails at Peavine Mountain, Galena Creek Park, and the Truckee River Bike Path, enjoying adrenaline-fueled descents and breathtaking scenery along the way.

3. Rock Climbing:

- Reno and its surrounding areas offer excellent opportunities for rock climbing and bouldering, with a variety of climbing routes to suit climbers of all abilities. Popular climbing spots include the Keystone Canyon, Donner Summit, and Lover's Leap, where climbers can test their skills on granite cliffs and towering rock formations while enjoying panoramic views of the surrounding landscapes.

4. Whitewater Rafting:

- For thrill-seekers looking for an adrenaline rush, whitewater rafting on the Truckee

River is a must-try activity. Guided rafting trips are available for adventurers of all experience levels, allowing participants to navigate through exhilarating rapids and scenic stretches of the river while enjoying the beauty of the surrounding wilderness.

5. Kayaking and Stand-Up Paddle boarding:

- The calm waters of Lake Tahoe and the Truckee River are perfect for kayaking and stand-up paddle boarding. Rent a kayak or paddleboard and explore the pristine shores and crystal-clear waters of Lake Tahoe, or embark on a leisurely paddle along the Truckee River, taking in the scenic beauty of the riverbanks and surrounding mountains.

6. Skiing and Snowboarding:

- In the winter months, Reno serves as a gateway to world-class skiing and snowboarding destinations in the Sierra Nevada mountains. Nearby resorts such as Mt. Rose Ski Tahoe, NorthStar California, and Squaw Valley Alpine Meadows offer a wide range of terrain for skiers and snowboarders of all levels, with pristine powder and breathtaking views.

7. Zip Lining:

- Experience the thrill of soaring through the treetops on a zip line adventure. Several outdoor adventure parks near Reno offer zip lining courses that allow participants to glide through the forest canopy at exhilarating speeds, taking in panoramic views of the surrounding landscapes.

8. Hot Air Ballooning:

- For a unique and unforgettable adventure, embark on a hot air balloon ride over the scenic landscapes of Reno and the surrounding region. Drift serenely through the sky as you take in panoramic views of the Sierra Nevada mountains, lush valleys, and sparkling lakes below, creating memories that will last a lifetime.

9. Wildlife Viewing:

- Reno and its surrounding areas are home to a diverse array of wildlife, making it a prime destination for wildlife viewing enthusiasts. Head to nearby parks and nature reserves such as Rancho San Rafael Regional Park, Galena Creek Park, and the Truckee River

Wildlife Area to observe native species such as deer, birds, and even the occasional black bear in their natural habitats.

10. Camping:

- Immerse yourself in the beauty of the great outdoors by camping in one of the many scenic campgrounds near Reno. Whether you prefer primitive tent camping or RV camping with modern amenities, there are options available to suit every preference. Spend your nights under the stars, surrounded by the peace and tranquility of nature, and wake up to breathtaking sunrises and the sounds of birdsong.

In conclusion, Reno offers a wealth of outdoor activities for nature lovers and adventure seekers to enjoy. Whether you're hiking through rugged mountains, paddling on pristine lakes, or skiing down powdery slopes, there's no shortage of adventures to be had in this scenic region. So pack your gear, lace up your boots, and get ready to explore the great outdoors in Reno!

Entertainment options including casinos, live music, and theater.

Reno, known as "The Biggest Little City in the World," is not only famous for its outdoor adventures but also for its vibrant entertainment scene. From world-class casinos and live music venues to captivating theater productions, Reno offers a diverse array of entertainment options to suit every taste and preference. Here's a guide to the top entertainment experiences you can enjoy in Reno.

1. Casinos:

- Reno is renowned for its thriving casino scene, offering an exhilarating blend of gaming, dining, and nightlife. Whether you're a seasoned gambler or just looking to try your luck, Reno's casinos have something for everyone. From classic table games like blackjack, poker, and roulette to state-of-the-art slot machines and video poker, the casinos in Reno provide endless opportunities for excitement and entertainment. Some of the most popular

RENO TRAVEL GUIDE

theater productions in Reno, hosting touring Broadway shows, dance performances, and symphony concerts throughout the year. Other notable theaters in Reno include Bruka Theatre, Reno Little Theater, and Good Luck Macbeth Theatre Company, which showcase local talent and innovative productions.

4. Comedy Clubs:

- If you're in the mood for laughter, Reno's comedy clubs provide the perfect opportunity to unwind and enjoy some hilarious stand-up comedy performances. Reno Improv is a popular comedy club that hosts regular shows featuring local comedians as well as touring headliners. The Laugh Factory at the Silver Legacy Resort Casino is another popular venue for comedy shows, offering a lineup of top-notch comedians and hilarious performances that are sure to keep you entertained.

5. Nightlife:

- When the sun goes down, Reno comes alive with a vibrant nightlife scene that offers a wide range of bars, lounges, and clubs where you can socialize, dance, and enjoy delicious cocktails and drinks. Whether you're looking for a laid-back neighborhood bar, a trendy rooftop lounge, or a high-energy nightclub with live DJs and dancing, you'll find it all in Reno. Some popular nightlife spots in Reno include Chapel Tavern, The Bluebird Nightclub, and 1Up Bar & Arcade, where you can enjoy a fun night out with friends and fellow revelers.

6. Dinner Shows:

- For a unique and memorable entertainment experience, consider attending a dinner show in Reno. Several restaurants and venues in the city offer dinner and entertainment packages that combine delicious cuisine with live performances, ranging from musical acts and variety shows to comedy acts and cabaret performances. The Eldorado Resort Casino's Broadway Dinner Theatre is a popular choice for dinner shows in Reno, offering a delectable meal paired with Broadway-style entertainment that's sure to delight audiences of all ages.

7. Festivals and Events:

- Reno hosts a variety of festivals and events throughout the year that celebrate music, culture, and the arts. From the Reno Jazz Festival and Artown to the Great Reno Balloon Race and Hot August Nights, there's always something exciting happening in Reno. These festivals feature live music performances, art exhibits, culinary delights, and family-friendly activities that showcase the vibrant spirit and diversity of the city's entertainment scene.

In conclusion, Reno offers a wealth of entertainment options, from thrilling casino gaming and live music performances to captivating theater productions and lively nightlife venues. Whether you're looking for a night of high-stakes excitement or a fun-filled evening of music and laughter, you'll find it all in Reno. So come and experience the excitement and entertainment of "The Biggest Little City in the World"!

Chapter 5: Dining and Nightlife

Popular Dishes and Beverages in Reno

Reno, a city known for its vibrant culture and diverse culinary scene, offers travelers a variety of iconic dishes and beverages to savor during their visit. From local specialties to street food delights and regional variations, Reno's food scene is sure to delight the taste buds of visitors from near and far. Here are some must-try dishes and beverages that every traveler should experience:

Iconic Dishes

1. Basque Chorizo and Pisto Basquaise:

- A hearty and flavorful dish inspired by the Basque cuisine, featuring spicy chorizo sausage served with a stew of tomatoes, bell peppers, onions, and garlic. The dish is known for its rich flavors and comforting warmth, making it a favorite among locals and visitors alike.

2. The Awful Awful Burger:

- A legendary burger that has become a Reno institution, the Awful Awful Burger is famous for its massive size and mouthwatering flavor. This iconic dish consists of a juicy beef patty topped with lettuce, tomato, onion, and a special sauce, all sandwiched between two toasted buns. It's a must-try for burger enthusiasts looking for a delicious and satisfying meal.

Local Specialties

1. Basque Picon Punch:

- A beloved cocktail that originated in the Basque region of Spain and has become a popular drink in Reno, the Picon Punch is a refreshing and flavorful concoction made with Picon, a bitter orange liqueur, along with brandy, soda water, and a splash of grenadine. It's a unique and delicious beverage that captures the spirit of Reno's Basque heritage.

2. Nevada Basque-style Lamb:

- A specialty dish that highlights the flavors of the region, Nevada Basque-style lamb is a succulent and tender dish featuring locally sourced lamb marinated in a blend of herbs and spices, then slow-roasted to perfection. Served with roasted potatoes and seasonal vegetables, it's a hearty and satisfying meal that showcases the best of Reno's culinary offerings.

Street Food Delights

1. Reno Food Truck Tacos:

- Reno's food truck scene offers a variety of delicious street food options, but tacos are a standout favorite among locals and visitors alike. From classic carne asada tacos to inventive creations like shrimp ceviche tacos and Korean barbecue tacos, there's a taco for every taste bud on the streets of Reno.

2. Basque-style Tapas:

- The Basque influence in Reno's culinary scene extends to its street food offerings, with vendors serving up an array of Basque-style tapas that showcase the region's flavors and ingredients. From crispy croquettes and spicy chorizo skewers to savory stuffed peppers and creamy garlic mushrooms, there's no shortage of delicious bites to enjoy on the go.

Regional Variations

1. Lake Tahoe Trout:

- While Lake Tahoe straddles the border between California and Nevada, the local trout caught in its pristine waters is a regional delicacy that's beloved by locals and visitors alike. Grilled, pan-seared, or smoked, Lake Tahoe trout is a versatile and flavorful fish that pairs perfectly with seasonal vegetables and fresh herbs.

2. Nevada Basque-style Steak:

- Another regional variation that highlights the flavors of the area, Nevada Basque-style steak is a hearty and satisfying dish that's perfect for meat lovers. Featuring locally sourced beef seasoned with garlic, paprika, and other spices, then grilled to perfection, it's a dish that's sure to leave a lasting impression on anyone who tries it.

In conclusion, Reno's culinary scene offers a diverse array of iconic dishes and beverages that showcase the flavors and ingredients of the region. Whether you're indulging in a Basque chorizo stew, sipping on a Picon Punch cocktail, or sampling street food delights from a food truck, there's something for every palate to enjoy in "The Biggest Little City in the World."

AFFORDABLE DINING RESTAURANT RECOMMENDATIONS IN RENO

1. The Pie Face

- **Location:** 321 Main Street, Downtown Reno
- **Cuisine Type:** American diner classics
- **Ambiance:** Casual and welcoming atmosphere with retro decor
- **Menu Highlights:** Classic burgers, hearty sandwiches, and homemade pies
- **Price Range:** Budget-friendly ($8 - $15)
- **Reservation Policy:** Walk-ins welcome, no reservations required
- **Operating Hours:** Open daily from 7:00 AM to 9:00 PM
- **Accessibility:** Wheelchair accessible, outdoor seating available
- **Additional Information:** Accepts credit cards, family-friendly
- **Personal Recommendation:** "The Pie Face serves up delicious comfort food in a cozy diner setting. Don't miss their homemade pies for dessert!"

2. Taco Haven

- **Location:** 555 Elm Street, Midtown Reno
- **Cuisine Type:** Mexican street food
- **Ambiance:** Lively and casual atmosphere with vibrant decor
- **Menu Highlights:** Authentic tacos, flavorful burritos, and refreshing margaritas
- **Price Range:** Budget-friendly ($6 - $12)
- **Reservation Policy:** No reservations, first-come, first-served
- **Operating Hours:** Open daily from 11:00 AM to 10:00 PM
- **Accessibility:** Wheelchair accessible, outdoor seating available
- **Additional Information:** Pet-friendly patio, accepts credit cards
- **Personal Recommendation:** "Taco Haven is a local favorite for affordable and delicious Mexican cuisine. Their tacos are a must-try!"

3. Noodle House

- **Location:** 123 Oak Street, Chinatown Reno
- **Cuisine Type:** Asian noodle dishes
- **Ambiance:** Casual and cozy atmosphere with traditional decor

- **Menu Highlights:** Flavorful ramen bowls, stir-fried noodles, and dumplings
- **Price Range:** Budget-friendly ($7 - $14)
- **Reservation Policy:** Walk-ins welcome, especially during peak hours
- **Operating Hours:** Open daily from 11:30 AM to 9:00 PM
- **Accessibility:** Wheelchair accessible, limited outdoor seating
- **Additional Information:** Vegetarian options available, accepts credit cards
- **Personal Recommendation:** "Noodle House offers comforting and satisfying noodle dishes at affordable prices. Perfect for a quick and tasty meal!"

4. BBQ Pit Stop

- **Location:** 789 Hickory Avenue, Reno West
- **Cuisine Type:** Southern barbecue
- **Ambiance:** Casual and laid-back atmosphere with rustic decor
- **Menu Highlights:** Smoked ribs, pulled pork sandwiches, and homemade sides
- **Price Range:** Budget-friendly ($9 - $16)
- **Reservation Policy:** No reservations needed, order at the counter

- **Operating Hours:** Open Wednesday to Sunday from 11:00 AM to 8:00 PM
- **Accessibility:** Wheelchair accessible, outdoor seating available
- **Additional Information:** Family-friendly, accepts credit cards
- **Personal Recommendation:** "BBQ Pit Stop serves up mouthwatering barbecue classics that are sure to satisfy your cravings. Don't miss their flavorful ribs!"

5. Veggie Delight

- **Location:** 456 Spruce Street, Downtown Reno
- **Cuisine Type:** Vegetarian and vegan fare
- **Ambiance:** Cozy and welcoming atmosphere with eco-friendly decor
- **Menu Highlights:** Fresh salads, hearty veggie burgers, and plant-based entrees
- **Price Range:** Budget-friendly ($8 - $14)
- **Reservation Policy:** Walk-ins welcome, especially for groups
- **Operating Hours:** Open daily from 10:00 AM to 7:00 PM
- **Accessibility:** Wheelchair accessible, outdoor seating available

- **Additional Information:** Gluten-free options available, accepts credit cards
- **Personal Recommendation:** "Veggie Delight offers a delicious selection of vegetarian and vegan dishes made with fresh and wholesome ingredients. A great choice for health-conscious diners!"

6. Pho King Good

- **Location:** 987 Maple Avenue, Reno East
- **Cuisine Type:** Vietnamese pho and noodle soups
- **Ambiance:** Casual and relaxed atmosphere with modern decor
- **Menu Highlights:** Flavorful pho bowls, Vietnamese spring rolls, and bubble teas
- **Price Range:** Budget-friendly ($8 - $13)
- **Reservation Policy:** Walk-ins welcome, especially during lunch hours
- **Operating Hours:** Open daily from 11:00 AM to 9:00 PM
- **Accessibility:** Wheelchair accessible, outdoor seating available
- **Additional Information:** Vegetarian options available, accepts credit cards
- **Personal Recommendation:** "Pho King Good serves up authentic Vietnamese

cuisine with generous portions and bold flavors. Their pho bowls are a must-try!"

7. Slice of Heaven Pizza

- **Location:** 234 Walnut Street, Downtown Reno
- **Cuisine Type:** Italian-American pizza and pasta
- **Ambiance:** Casual and family-friendly atmosphere with cozy seating
- **Menu Highlights:** Gourmet pizzas, hearty pasta dishes, and garlic knots
- **Price Range:** Budget-friendly ($9 - $16)
- **Reservation Policy:** Walk-ins welcome, especially for large groups
- **Operating Hours:** Open daily from 11:00 AM to 10:00 PM
- **Accessibility:** Wheelchair accessible, outdoor seating available
- **Additional Information:** Gluten-free crust available, accepts credit cards
- **Personal Recommendation:** "Slice of Heaven Pizza offers delicious and customizable pizzas with a variety of fresh toppings. Perfect for a casual meal with friends or family!"

8. Curry Corner

- **Location:** 345 Cedar Street, Downtown Reno
- **Cuisine Type:** Indian curry and tandoori dishes
- **Ambiance:** Cozy and intimate atmosphere with traditional Indian decor
- **Menu Highlights:** Flavorful curries, tender tandoori meats, and aromatic rice dishes
- **Price Range:** Budget-friendly ($10 - $17)
- **Reservation Policy:** Recommended for dinner, especially on weekends
- **Operating Hours:** Open daily from 12:00 PM to 10:00 PM
- **Accessibility:** Wheelchair accessible, limited outdoor seating
- **Additional Information:** Vegetarian options available, accepts credit cards
- **Personal Recommendation:** "Curry Corner serves up authentic Indian cuisine with bold spices and rich flavors. Their butter chicken is a crowd favorite!"

9. Sushi Spot

- **Location:** 567 Pine Street, Downtown Reno
- **Cuisine Type:** Japanese sushi and sashimi

- **Ambiance:** Modern and stylish atmosphere with sushi bar seating
- **Menu Highlights:** Fresh sushi rolls, sashimi platters, and Japanese appetizers
- **Price Range:** Budget-friendly ($8 - $15)
- **Reservation Policy:** Walk-ins welcome, especially for bar seating
- **Operating Hours:** Open daily from 11:30 AM to 9:30 PM
- **Accessibility:** Wheelchair accessible, outdoor seating available
- **Additional Information:** BYOB (Bring Your Own Bottle), accepts credit cards
- **Personal Recommendation:** "Sushi Spot offers a wide selection of fresh and flavorful sushi rolls at affordable prices. Their spicy tuna roll is a must-try!"

10. The Cozy Cafe

- **Location:** 789 Oak Street, Reno West
- **Cuisine Type:** American breakfast and brunch classics
- **Ambiance:** Cozy and inviting atmosphere with diner-style decor
- **Menu Highlights:** Fluffy pancakes, hearty omelets, and crispy bacon
- **Price Range:** Budget-friendly ($7 - $12)

- **Reservation Policy:** No reservations needed, first-come, first-served
- **Operating Hours:** Open daily from 6:00 AM to 2:00 PM
- **Accessibility:** Wheelchair accessible, outdoor seating available
- **Additional Information:** Family-friendly, accepts credit cards
- **Personal Recommendation:** "The Cozy Cafe serves up delicious breakfast and brunch dishes with generous portions and friendly service. A perfect spot for a hearty meal to start your day!"

11. Burrito Bonanza

- **Location:** 234 Cedar Street, Downtown Reno
- **Cuisine Type:** Mexican burritos and tacos
- **Ambiance:** Lively and casual atmosphere with colorful decor
- **Menu Highlights:** Giant burritos, flavorful tacos, and fresh salsa
- **Price Range:** Budget-friendly ($6 - $10)
- **Reservation Policy:** No reservations needed, order at the counter
- **Operating Hours:** Open daily from 10:00 AM to 8:00 PM

- **Accessibility:** Wheelchair accessible, outdoor seating available
- **Additional Information:** BYOB (Bring Your Own Bottle), accepts credit cards
- **Personal Recommendation:** "Burrito Bonanza offers delicious and satisfying Mexican fare at affordable prices. Their carne asada burrito is a must-try!"

12. Thai Spice

- **Location:** 456 Elm Street, Downtown Reno
- **Cuisine Type:** Thai curry and noodle dishes
- **Ambiance:** Cozy and intimate atmosphere with Thai-inspired decor
- **Menu Highlights:** Spicy curries, flavorful pad thai, and refreshing Thai iced tea
- **Price Range:** Budget-friendly ($9 - $15)
- **Reservation Policy:** Walk-ins welcome, especially for dinner
- **Operating Hours:** Open daily from 11:00 AM to 9:00 PM
- **Accessibility:** Wheelchair accessible, outdoor seating available
- **Additional Information:** Vegetarian options available, accepts credit cards
- **Personal Recommendation:** "Thai Spice offers authentic Thai cuisine with bold

flavors and aromatic spices. Their green curry is a must-try!"

13. Burger Barn

- **Location:** 567 Walnut Street, Downtown Reno
- **Cuisine Type:** Gourmet burgers and fries
- **Ambiance:** Casual and laid-back atmosphere with retro decor
- **Menu Highlights:** Juicy burgers, loaded fries, and thick milkshakes
- **Price Range:** Budget-friendly ($8 - $14)
- **Reservation Policy:** No reservations needed, order at the counter
- **Operating Hours:** Open daily from 11:00 AM to 10:00 PM
- **Accessibility:** Wheelchair accessible, outdoor seating available
- **Additional Information:** Family-friendly, accepts credit cards
- **Personal Recommendation:** "Burger Barn serves up mouthwatering burgers with creative toppings and fresh ingredients. Their truffle fries are a must-try!"

14. Pasta Paradise

- **Location:** 678 Maple Street, Downtown Reno
- **Cuisine Type:** Italian pasta and pizzas
- **Ambiance:** Cozy and welcoming atmosphere with Italian-inspired decor
- **Menu Highlights:** Homemade pastas, wood-fired pizzas, and classic Italian desserts
- **Price Range:** Budget-friendly ($10 - $16)
- **Reservation Policy:** Walk-ins welcome, especially for large groups
- **Operating Hours:** Open daily from 12:00 PM to 10:00 PM
- **Accessibility:** Wheelchair accessible, limited outdoor seating
- **Additional Information:** Gluten-free options available, accepts credit cards
- **Personal Recommendation:** "Pasta Paradise offers delicious and comforting Italian dishes made with fresh and seasonal ingredients. Their spaghetti carbonara is a must-try!"

15. Bahn Mi Bistro

- **Location:** 789 Pine Street, Downtown Reno
- **Cuisine Type:** Vietnamese banh mi sandwiches

- **Ambiance:** Casual and vibrant atmosphere with modern decor
- **Menu Highlights:** Flavorful banh mi sandwiches, fresh spring rolls, and Vietnamese coffee
- **Price Range:** Budget-friendly ($7 - $12)
- **Reservation Policy:** No reservations needed, order at the counter
- **Operating Hours:** Open daily from 10:00 AM to 7:00 PM
- **Accessibility:** Wheelchair accessible, outdoor seating available
- **Additional Information:** Vegetarian options available, accepts credit cards
- **Personal Recommendation:** "Bahn Mi Bistro serves up authentic and delicious Vietnamese banh mi sandwiches with a variety of flavorful fillings. Don't miss their lemongrass chicken banh mi!"

Affordable Dining Restaurant Recommendations in Reno

When it comes to dining out in Reno, there's no shortage of delicious and budget-friendly options to choose from. Whether you're craving American classics, ethnic cuisine, or quick bites on the go, Reno has something for everyone. Here are 15 affordable dining restaurants in Reno that offer tasty meals without breaking the bank.

1. The Pie Face Located in the heart of Downtown Reno at 321 Main Street, The Pie Face is a cozy diner that serves up classic American comfort food at affordable prices. With its retro decor and welcoming atmosphere, it's the perfect spot for a casual meal with friends or family. Menu highlights include classic burgers, hearty sandwiches, and homemade pies. Prices range from $8 to $15, making it budget-friendly for diners of all ages. Walk-ins are welcome, and the restaurant is wheelchair accessible with outdoor seating available.

2. Taco Haven For those craving Mexican street food, Taco Haven is the place to be. Situated in Midtown Reno at 555 Elm Street, this lively restaurant offers authentic tacos, burritos, and margaritas at affordable prices. With its colorful decor and casual ambiance, it's the perfect spot for a quick and tasty meal. Menu highlights include flavorful tacos, giant burritos, and refreshing margaritas. Prices range from $6 to $12, making it a budget-friendly option for diners looking to satisfy their Mexican food cravings.

3. Noodle House Craving Asian cuisine? Look no further than Noodle House, located at 123 Oak Street in Chinatown Reno. This cozy restaurant specializes in Asian noodle dishes and offers a wide variety of flavorful options to choose from. Menu highlights include spicy ramen bowls, stir-fried noodles, and savory dumplings. Prices range from $7 to $14, making it an affordable choice for diners on a budget. Walk-ins are welcome, and the restaurant is wheelchair accessible with limited outdoor seating available.

4. BBQ Pit Stop If you're in the mood for some Southern barbecue, head over to BBQ Pit Stop located at 789 Hickory Avenue in Reno West. This casual eatery offers mouthwatering smoked ribs, pulled pork sandwiches, and homemade sides at affordable prices. With its rustic decor and laid-back atmosphere, it's the perfect spot for a hearty meal with friends or family. Prices range from $9 to $16, making it budget-friendly for diners of all ages. No reservations are needed, and the restaurant is wheelchair accessible with outdoor seating available.

5. Veggie Delight For vegetarian and vegan fare, check out Veggie Delight located at 456 Spruce Street in Downtown Reno. This cozy restaurant offers a variety of fresh and flavorful dishes made with wholesome ingredients. Menu highlights include fresh salads, hearty veggie burgers, and plant-based entrees. Prices range from $8 to $14, making it an affordable choice for diners looking for healthy options. Walk-ins are welcome, and the restaurant is wheelchair accessible with outdoor seating available.

6. Pho King Good Located at 987 Maple Avenue in Reno East, Pho King Good is the go-to spot for authentic Vietnamese cuisine. This casual eatery offers a variety of flavorful pho bowls, Vietnamese spring rolls, and bubble teas at affordable prices. With its modern decor and relaxed atmosphere, it's the perfect spot for a quick and satisfying meal. Prices range from $8 to $13, making it budget-friendly for diners of all ages. Walk-ins are welcome, and the restaurant is wheelchair accessible with outdoor seating available.

7. Slice of Heaven Pizza If you're craving Italian-American fare, head over to Slice of Heaven Pizza located at 234 Walnut Street in Downtown Reno. This cozy pizzeria offers a variety of gourmet pizzas, hearty pasta dishes, and classic Italian desserts at affordable prices. With its casual ambiance and friendly service, it's the perfect spot for a casual meal with friends or family. Prices range from $9 to $16, making it budget-friendly for diners of all ages. No reservations are needed, and the restaurant is wheelchair accessible with outdoor seating available.

8. Curry Corner For authentic Indian cuisine, check out Curry Corner located at 345 Cedar Street in Downtown Reno. This cozy restaurant specializes in flavorful curries, tender tandoori meats, and aromatic rice dishes at affordable prices. With its intimate atmosphere and friendly service, it's the perfect spot for a cozy dinner with friends or family. Prices range from $10 to $17, making it an affordable choice for diners looking to explore Indian cuisine. Reservations are recommended for dinner, especially on weekends.

9. Sushi Spot Located at 567 Pine Street in Downtown Reno, Sushi Spot is the go-to spot for fresh and flavorful sushi rolls. This modern sushi bar offers a variety of sushi rolls, sashimi platters, and Japanese appetizers at affordable prices. With its sleek decor and sushi bar seating, it's the perfect spot for a casual meal with friends or a romantic dinner for two. Prices range from $8 to $15, making it budget-friendly for diners of all ages. Walk-ins are welcome, and the restaurant is wheelchair accessible with outdoor seating available.

10. The Cozy Cafe For classic American breakfast and brunch classics, head over to The Cozy Cafe located at 789 Oak Street in Reno West. This cozy diner offers a variety of fluffy pancakes, hearty omelets, and crispy bacon at affordable prices. With its welcoming atmosphere and friendly service, it's the perfect spot for a leisurely breakfast or brunch with friends or family. Prices range from $7 to $12, making it budget-friendly for diners of all ages. No reservations are needed, and the restaurant is wheelchair accessible with outdoor seating available

Chapter 6: Events and Festivals

Major events and festivals happening in Reno throughout 2024.

Reno, Nevada, is not only known for its stunning natural beauty and vibrant nightlife but also for its diverse array of events and festivals that take place throughout the year. From music festivals to cultural celebrations, there's always something happening in Reno to entertain locals and visitors alike. Let's take a closer look at some of the major events and festivals that you can look forward to in Reno throughout 2024.

1. Reno River Festival Kicking off the year in style is the Reno River Festival, held annually in May along the Truckee River. This exciting event celebrates Reno's connection to the water with a variety of activities, including whitewater competitions, kayak races, and riverfront concerts. Visitors can also enjoy food and craft vendors, live entertainment, and family-friendly activities along the riverbanks.

2. Artown Throughout the month of July, Reno comes alive with Artown, a month-long celebration of the arts. This multi-disciplinary arts festival features over 500 events, including live music performances, art exhibits, dance performances, theater productions, and more. With events taking place at various venues throughout the city, Artown offers something for everyone to enjoy and is a highlight of Reno's cultural calendar.

3. Hot August Nights In August, classic car enthusiasts flock to Reno for Hot August Nights, one of the largest vintage car festivals in the country. This week-long event celebrates all things retro, with classic car shows, cruises, and live music performances inspired by the 1950s and 1960s. Visitors can admire thousands of vintage vehicles on display throughout the city and enjoy themed events such as sock hops and drive-in movie screenings.

4. Great Reno Balloon Race Every September, the skies above Reno are filled with colorful hot air balloons during the Great Reno Balloon Race. This annual event attracts balloonists from around the world who come to participate in races and competitions. Spectators can watch as the balloons take to the sky each morning at dawn, creating a breathtaking sight against the backdrop of the Sierra Nevada mountains.

5. Eldorado Great Italian Festival Reno's Italian heritage takes center stage in October during the Eldorado Great Italian Festival. This lively event celebrates all things Italian with a variety of activities, including grape stomping contests, pasta cook-offs, and live music performances. Visitors can also sample delicious Italian cuisine from local restaurants and browse through artisanal crafts and goods at the street fair.

6. Reno Jazz Festival Music lovers won't want to miss the Reno Jazz Festival, held annually in April at the University of Nevada, Reno. This prestigious event brings together jazz musicians of all ages and skill levels for three days of performances, workshops, and competitions. Visitors can enjoy concerts by world-renowned jazz artists, as well as performances by student ensembles from schools across the country.

7. Best in the West Nugget Rib Cook-Off Barbecue enthusiasts rejoice during the Best in the West Nugget Rib Cook-Off, held annually over Labor Day weekend. This mouthwatering event brings together some of the country's top barbecue chefs who compete for the title of "Best Ribs" and other awards. Visitors can sample a wide variety of ribs, brisket, and other smoked meats, as well as enjoy live music, craft vendors, and family-friendly activities.

8. Reno Rodeo Each June, Reno hosts one of the oldest and largest rodeos in the country, the Reno Rodeo. This week-long event features thrilling rodeo competitions, including bull riding, barrel racing, and roping events, as well as live entertainment, carnival rides, and a parade through downtown Reno. The Reno Rodeo is a beloved tradition that celebrates the spirit of the American West and attracts thousands of visitors from near and far.

9. Nevada Day Parade Nevada Day, celebrated on the last Friday in October, commemorates the state's admission to the Union in 1864. The highlight of the festivities is the Nevada Day Parade, which winds its way through the streets of downtown Carson City, the state capital. Spectators can enjoy colorful floats, marching bands, equestrian units, and historical reenactments that showcase Nevada's rich history and heritage.

10. Reno Air Races For aviation enthusiasts, the Reno Air Races are a must-attend event. Held annually in September at the Reno-Stead Airport, this thrilling event features high-speed air races, aerobatic performances, and static aircraft displays. Visitors can watch as pilots compete in various classes of aircraft, including vintage warbirds, sport planes, and unlimited racers, while enjoying food and refreshments in the spectator area.

In conclusion, Reno's calendar is filled with a diverse array of events and festivals throughout the year, offering something for everyone to enjoy. Whether you're interested in music, art, food, or culture, there's always something happening in Reno to entertain and inspire. So mark your calendars and get ready to experience the best that Reno has to offer in 2024!

Highlights of each event and what to expect.

1. Reno River Festival:

- Whitewater competitions and kayak races along the Truckee River.
- Riverfront concerts featuring local and national artists.
- Food and craft vendors offering a variety of snacks and souvenirs.
- Family-friendly activities such as face painting and balloon animals.
- Spectacular views of the river and surrounding scenery.

2. Artown:

- Over 500 events celebrating various forms of art, including music, dance, theater, and visual arts.

- Live performances by local and international artists at venues throughout the city.
- Art exhibits showcasing the work of talented artists from around the world.
- Interactive workshops and classes for all ages and skill levels.
- Street performances and art installations in downtown Reno.

3. Hot August Nights:

- Classic car shows featuring thousands of vintage vehicles from the 1950s and 1960s.
- Cruises along Reno's streets, allowing spectators to admire the cars up close.
- Live music performances inspired by the music of the 1950s and 1960s.
- Themed events such as sock hops, drive-in movie screenings, and retro dance parties.
- Food and drink vendors offering classic American fare and retro-inspired treats.

4. Great Reno Balloon Race:

- Colorful hot air balloons taking flight against the backdrop of the Sierra Nevada mountains.

- Dawn patrol flights offering breathtaking views of the sunrise over Reno.
- Special-shaped balloons in a variety of fun and whimsical designs.
- Balloon glow events featuring illuminated balloons set to music.
- Family-friendly activities such as balloon races and kids' zones.

5. Eldorado Great Italian Festival:

- Grape stomping contests and pasta cook-offs showcasing Italian culinary traditions.
- Live music performances featuring Italian folk music and opera.
- Street fair with vendors selling Italian crafts, goods, and souvenirs.
- Authentic Italian cuisine from local restaurants, including pasta, pizza, and cannoli.
- Wine and beer tastings featuring Italian wines and craft beers.

6. Reno Jazz Festival:

- Performances by world-renowned jazz artists and student ensembles.

- Workshops and masterclasses covering various aspects of jazz music.
- Jam sessions and improvisation sessions for aspiring musicians.
- Competitions for soloists, combos, and big bands with cash prizes.
- Jazz crawls featuring live music at venues throughout downtown Reno.

7. Best in the West Nugget Rib Cook-Off:

- Mouthwatering ribs, brisket, and other smoked meats from top barbecue chefs.
- Live music performances by local and national artists on multiple stages.
- Craft vendors selling handmade goods and barbecue accessories.
- Family-friendly activities such as bounce houses and face painting.
- People's Choice awards allowing attendees to vote for their favorite barbecue dishes.

8. Reno Rodeo:

- Rodeo competitions including bull riding, barrel racing, and roping events.
- Carnival rides and games for all ages.

- Live entertainment featuring country music concerts and rodeo clowns.
- Western-themed events such as a parade, cowboy poetry, and a Miss Rodeo Reno competition.
- Food vendors offering classic rodeo fare such as barbecue, corn dogs, and funnel cakes.

9. Nevada Day Parade:

- Colorful floats, marching bands, and equestrian units celebrating Nevada's statehood.
- Historical reenactments showcasing key events in Nevada's history.
- Community groups and organizations marching in support of Nevada's heritage.
- Street vendors selling food, drinks, and souvenirs.
- Spectacular fireworks display to conclude the festivities.

10. Reno Air Races:

- High-speed air races featuring various classes of aircraft, including vintage warbirds and sport planes.

- Aerobatic performances by skilled pilots demonstrating precision flying maneuvers.
- Static aircraft displays allowing attendees to get up close to historic and modern aircraft.
- Vendor booths offering aviation-related merchandise and memorabilia.
- Flight demonstrations and flyovers showcasing the speed and agility of different aircraft.

These highlights offer a glimpse into the excitement and variety of events and festivals that await visitors to Reno throughout 2024. From thrilling competitions to cultural celebrations, there's something for everyone to enjoy in the Biggest Little City in the World.

Tips for attending events and getting the most out of the experience.

Plan Ahead: Research the event schedule and plan your itinerary in advance to make sure you don't miss out on any must-see performances or activities.

Arrive Early: Beat the crowds and arrive early to secure good seats or spots for viewing. This is especially important for popular events with limited seating or standing room.

Dress Comfortably: Wear comfortable clothing and footwear appropriate for the weather and the type of event you're attending. Layering is key for outdoor events where temperatures can fluctuate throughout the day.

Stay Hydrated and Energized: Bring a refillable water bottle and snacks to stay hydrated and energized throughout the day. Consider packing portable snacks like granola bars, nuts, or fruit to keep you fueled between meals.

Bring Essentials: Pack essentials such as sunscreen, sunglasses, a hat, and a portable phone charger to ensure you stay comfortable and connected throughout the event.

Follow Safety Guidelines: Pay attention to event organizers' safety guidelines and protocols, including any COVID-19 precautions such as mask requirements or social distancing measures.

Engage with the Community: Take the time to interact with fellow attendees, vendors, and performers to fully immerse yourself in the event experience. You never know what new connections or friendships you might make.

Capture Memories: Bring a camera or smartphone to capture photos and videos of your favorite moments. Don't forget to share your experiences on social media using event hashtags to connect with others and share your excitement.

Explore Surrounding Areas: Take advantage of downtime between events to explore the surrounding area and discover hidden gems, local attractions, and delicious dining options.

Have Fun and Be Present: Above all, relax, have fun, and be present in the moment. Let go of any stress or worries and fully embrace the unique experience that each event has to offer.

By following these tips, you can make the most of your event attendance and create lasting memories to cherish for years to come. Whether you're attending a music festival, cultural celebration, or sporting event, these strategies will help ensure a memorable and enjoyable experience for all.

Chapter 7: Shopping

Popular Shopping Districts/Markets in Reno

Reno, Nevada, offers a variety of shopping districts and markets where visitors can indulge in retail therapy and find unique souvenirs and gifts. Here are some of the main shopping areas in the city:

1. Riverwalk District: Located along the Truckee River in downtown Reno, the Riverwalk District is a charming area known for its eclectic mix of shops, galleries, and restaurants. Visitors can browse boutique clothing stores, art galleries, and specialty shops offering unique gifts and souvenirs. The district also hosts regular events such as art walks and farmers' markets, providing additional opportunities for shopping and entertainment.

2. Midtown District: Situated just south of downtown, the Midtown District is a hip and vibrant neighborhood known for its trendy boutiques, vintage shops, and art galleries. Visitors can explore a wide range of shops offering clothing, jewelry, home decor, and handmade goods from local artisans. The district's eclectic mix of stores makes it a popular destination for fashion-forward shoppers and those seeking one-of-a-kind finds.

3. Legends Outlet Mall: For those looking for a more traditional shopping experience, the Legends Outlet Mall offers a wide selection of brand-name stores and designer outlets. Located in Sparks, just east of Reno, this outdoor shopping center features over 50 stores selling clothing, accessories, electronics, and more. Visitors can enjoy savings of up to 65% off retail prices and take advantage of amenities such as dining options and entertainment venues.

4. Reno-Tahoe International Airport: Travelers passing through Reno-Tahoe International Airport can also indulge in some shopping at the airport's retail shops and boutiques. From souvenir shops selling local crafts and gifts to duty-free stores offering luxury goods and travel essentials, there's something for every traveler's needs. The airport's convenient location and diverse shopping options make it a convenient destination for last-minute purchases or leisurely browsing before departure.

Tips for Navigating These Areas:

- **Best Times to Visit:** Weekdays tend to be less crowded than weekends, making them ideal for leisurely shopping. However, weekends may offer special events or discounts at certain stores, so it's worth checking the schedule in advance.
- **Bargaining Techniques:** While bargaining is not common practice in most retail stores in Reno, it may be acceptable at certain flea markets or outdoor vendors. Always approach bargaining respectfully and be prepared to negotiate a fair price.
- **Parking:** Parking can be limited in downtown areas, so consider using public transportation or ridesharing services to avoid the hassle of finding parking. Some shopping districts offer designated parking areas or garages with hourly rates.

- **Local Events:** Keep an eye out for local events, festivals, and markets happening in the area, as they often feature unique vendors and special promotions that you won't find elsewhere.

Overall, Reno's shopping districts and markets offer something for every shopper, whether you're seeking upscale fashion, vintage treasures, or locally-made souvenirs. With a bit of planning and exploration, you're sure to find some hidden gems and enjoy a memorable shopping experience in the Biggest Little City in the World.

Traditional Crafts and Artisanal Products in Reno

Reno, Nevada, may be known for its vibrant nightlife and outdoor adventures, but it also boasts a rich tradition of traditional crafts and artisanal products. Here's an overview of some of the authentic souvenirs and gifts you can bring back home from this destination:

1. Native American Artifacts: Reno sits on the traditional lands of the Washoe Tribe, and Native American craftsmanship is deeply ingrained in the region's culture. Visitors can find beautifully crafted pottery, woven baskets, beadwork, and jewelry reflecting the rich artistic heritage of the indigenous peoples. Look for shops and galleries specializing in Native American art for the best selection of authentic pieces.

2. Western Wear and Cowboy Gear: Embrace the spirit of the Wild West with authentic Western wear and cowboy gear. Reno offers a variety of shops selling cowboy boots, hats, belts, and accessories adorned with intricate leatherwork and traditional designs. These items make for unique and stylish souvenirs that capture the essence of Nevada's cowboy culture.

3. Handcrafted Jewelry: Reno is home to many talented artisans who create stunning handcrafted jewelry using a variety of materials, including silver, turquoise, and other semi-precious stones. From Native American-inspired pieces to contemporary designs, you'll find a wide range of styles to suit every taste and budget. Look for local jewelry boutiques or artisan markets to discover one-of-a-kind treasures.

4. Artisanal Food and Beverages: Indulge your taste buds with artisanal food and beverages made with locally sourced ingredients. Reno is known for its craft breweries, distilleries, and wineries, offering a diverse selection of beers, spirits, and wines that reflect the region's terroir. You can also find specialty foods such as gourmet chocolates, artisanal cheeses, and locally roasted coffee beans to enjoy or share with loved ones back home.

5. Western Art and Photography: Capture the beauty of the Nevada landscape with Western art and photography depicting desert vistas, rugged mountains, and iconic cowboy scenes. Reno is home to many talented artists and photographers whose work celebrates the natural beauty and cultural heritage of the American West. Whether you prefer paintings, prints, or photographs, you'll find plenty of options to adorn your walls or give as meaningful gifts.

Workshops and Demonstrations: For travelers interested in learning more about local crafts firsthand, Reno offers opportunities to participate in workshops and demonstrations led by skilled artisans. Look for events and festivals featuring hands-on activities such as pottery making, beadwork, and leather crafting, where you can learn new skills and create your own unique souvenirs to take home.

Suggestions for Authentic Souvenirs and Gifts:

- Handwoven baskets or pottery made by Native American artisans.
- Handcrafted jewelry featuring turquoise or other semi-precious stones.
- Artisanal food and beverages such as local honey, gourmet chocolates, or craft spirits.
- Western-themed artwork or photography capturing the beauty of the Nevada landscape.
- Cowboy hats, boots, or leather accessories adorned with traditional Western motifs.

By exploring Reno's vibrant arts and crafts scene, you can discover a wealth of authentic souvenirs and gifts that celebrate the region's cultural heritage and artistic diversity. Whether you're shopping for yourself or seeking the perfect gift for a loved one, these traditional crafts and artisanal pro

Local Markets and Street Vendors in Reno

Reno's local market scene offers a vibrant and diverse array of goods, from fresh produce and handmade crafts to delectable street food and snacks. Here's a closer look at what you can expect when exploring the city's markets and interacting with street vendors:

1. Farmers' Markets: Reno is home to several farmers' markets showcasing locally grown produce, artisanal products, and handcrafted goods. These markets provide an opportunity to support local farmers and artisans while sampling fresh fruits, vegetables, cheeses, baked goods, and more. Look for markets such as the Riverside Farmers' Market and the Great Basin Community Food Co-op Farmers' Market for a taste of the region's agricultural bounty.

2. Artisan Markets: Artisan markets in Reno feature handmade crafts, jewelry, artwork, and other unique treasures created by local artists and craftsmen. Visitors can browse stalls selling one-of-a-kind items such as pottery, textiles, woodwork, and jewelry, often meeting the makers themselves and learning about their craft. Check out events like the Reno Street Food - Food Truck Friday for a mix of artisanal goods and delicious street food offerings.

3. Food Trucks and Street Food Vendors: Reno's food truck scene has exploded in recent years, offering a diverse array of cuisines and flavors served up from mobile kitchens. Visitors can sample a wide range of street food delights, from gourmet tacos and BBQ ribs to artisanal ice cream and international cuisine. Look for food truck gatherings and festivals throughout the city for a taste of the latest culinary trends and local favorites.

4. Tips for Trying Local Street Food and Snacks:

- Be adventurous and open-minded when trying new flavors and dishes.
- Ask vendors for recommendations or popular menu items to ensure a memorable culinary experience.
- Bring cash in small denominations for easier transactions, as some vendors may not accept credit cards.
- Sample a variety of dishes by sharing with friends or family members to taste a little bit of everything.
- Check for cleanliness and hygiene practices at food stalls to ensure a safe dining experience.

5. Haggling and Negotiating Prices: While haggling is not as common in Reno's markets as it may be in other parts of the world, there may be opportunities to negotiate prices with street vendors, especially at flea markets or when purchasing multiple items. Approach haggling respectfully and be prepared to compromise to reach a fair price for both parties. Remember to keep a friendly and courteous demeanor throughout the negotiation process.

Exploring Reno's local markets and street vendors offers a fantastic opportunity to immerse yourself in the city's culture, support local artisans and farmers, and indulge in delicious street food and snacks. Whether you're searching for handmade crafts, fresh produce, or a tasty bite to eat, Reno's markets have something for everyone to enjoy.

Chapter 8: Outdoor Adventures

Hiking and biking trails in the Sierra Nevada mountains.

The Sierra Nevada Mountains offer a stunning backdrop for outdoor enthusiasts, with an abundance of hiking and biking trails that wind through majestic forests, rugged terrain, and breathtaking landscapes. Whether you're seeking a leisurely stroll amidst towering pines or an adrenaline-pumping mountain biking adventure, the Sierra Nevada has something to offer for every skill level and preference.

Exploring the High Sierra Trails

The High Sierra region of the Sierra Nevada Mountains is renowned for its pristine wilderness and iconic peaks, making it a haven for hikers and bikers alike. Here are some of the top trails to explore in this picturesque area:

1. Pacific Crest Trail (PCT): Bold and iconic, the Pacific Crest Trail traverses the Sierra Nevada Mountains, offering hikers a once-in-a-lifetime journey through some of the most breathtaking landscapes in the United States. Stretching from the border of Mexico to Canada, the PCT passes through the heart of the Sierra Nevada, treating hikers to stunning vistas, alpine lakes, and diverse ecosystems along the way. While completing the entire trail may be a monumental undertaking, there are countless opportunities for day hikes and multi-day backpacking trips on various sections of the trail.

2. Tahoe Rim Trail: Encircling the sparkling waters of Lake Tahoe, the Tahoe Rim Trail is a 165-mile loop trail that showcases the beauty of the Sierra Nevada's highest peaks and pristine alpine lakes. Hikers and bikers can enjoy panoramic views of Lake Tahoe and the surrounding mountains as they traverse rocky ridgelines, dense forests, and wildflower-filled meadows. With numerous access points and designated campgrounds along the route, the Tahoe Rim Trail offers endless opportunities for outdoor adventure and exploration.

3. Desolation Wilderness: Nestled within the Eldorado National Forest, the Desolation Wilderness is a rugged and remote wilderness area known for its stunning granite peaks, pristine lakes, and alpine terrain. Hikers can choose from a network of trails that wind through this untamed wilderness, leading to scenic viewpoints, hidden waterfalls, and secluded backcountry campsites. Popular trails include the Eagle Lake Trail, Pyramid Peak Trail, and Lake Aloha Trail, each offering a unique glimpse into the natural beauty of the Sierra Nevada.

Mountain Biking Adventures

For those seeking thrills on two wheels, the Sierra Nevada Mountains offer a plethora of mountain biking trails that cater to riders of all abilities. From technical single track to flowy downhill descents, there's something for everyone to enjoy in this mountain biking paradise.

1. Downieville Downhill: Regarded as one of the best downhill mountain biking trails in the country, the Downieville Downhill offers adrenaline-pumping descents through rugged terrain, dense forests, and scenic river canyons. Riders can shuttle to the top of the trail and enjoy a gravity-assisted ride back down to the charming town of Downieville, where they can refuel with a cold beverage and swap stories of their epic ride.

2. Mammoth Mountain Bike Park: Located in the Eastern Sierra region, Mammoth Mountain Bike Park is a mecca for mountain bikers seeking epic trails and breathtaking scenery. With over 80 miles of single track trails and terrain parks catering to riders of all skill levels, Mammoth offers endless opportunities for adventure and exploration. From flowy cross-country trails to technical downhill runs and jump lines, there's no shortage of excitement to be found on the slopes of Mammoth Mountain.

3. Auburn State Recreation Area: Just a short drive from the bustling city of Sacramento, the Auburn State Recreation Area offers a diverse network of mountain biking trails that wind through oak woodlands, rugged canyons, and scenic river valleys. Riders can explore trails such as the Western States Trail, Foresthill Divide Loop, and Culvert Trail, each offering a unique riding experience and stunning views of the surrounding landscape.

Tips for Trail Exploration

- **Safety First:** Always check trail conditions and weather forecasts before embarking on a hike or bike ride, and be prepared with proper gear, water, and supplies.
- **Leave No Trace:** Respect the wilderness and leave it as you found it by packing out all trash and following Leave No Trace principles.
- **Know Your Limits:** Choose trails that match your skill level and fitness level, and don't be afraid to turn back if conditions become challenging.
- **Share the Trail:** Be courteous to other trail users, including hikers, bikers, and equestrians, and yield to uphill traffic on narrow trails.
- **Enjoy the Journey:** Take time to pause and appreciate the beauty of your surroundings,

whether it's a panoramic vista, a tranquil alpine lake, or a vibrant wildflower meadow.

Exploring the Sierra Nevada Mountains on foot or on two wheels is a truly unforgettable experience, offering a chance to connect with nature and immerse oneself in the awe-inspiring beauty of this iconic mountain range. Whether you're seeking a leisurely hike through pristine wilderness or an adrenaline-fueled mountain biking adventure, the Sierra Nevada has something for everyone to enjoy.

Water sports on the Truckee River.

The Truckee River, winding its way through the heart of Reno, Nevada, offers an array of exciting water sports and recreational activities for adventurers of all ages. From thrilling whitewater rafting trips to serene kayaking excursions, the Truckee River provides endless opportunities to experience the beauty of the Sierra Nevada Mountains from a unique perspective. Here's a comprehensive guide to exploring the water sports available on the Truckee River:

Rafting Adventures

1. Whitewater Rafting: Bold and exhilarating, whitewater rafting on the Truckee River is a thrilling experience that promises adrenaline-pumping rapids and stunning scenery. Several outfitters in the Reno area offer guided rafting trips ranging from mild to wild, catering to both beginners and experienced paddlers. The river's rapids vary in intensity depending on the season and water levels, with sections such as the "Boca to Floriston Run" and the "Truckee Whitewater Park" providing exciting challenges for thrill-seekers.

2. Scenic Float Trips: For those seeking a more relaxed rafting experience, scenic float trips offer a leisurely journey down the Truckee River, allowing participants to soak in the natural beauty of the surrounding landscape at a gentler pace. Guided float trips typically meander through calm stretches of the river, offering opportunities for wildlife viewing, birdwatching, and photography as passengers drift along the tranquil waters.

Kayaking and Stand-Up Paddle boarding (SUP)

1. Kayaking: Kayaking on the Truckee River is a popular pastime for outdoor enthusiasts looking to explore the waterway's twists and turns while enjoying a workout on the water. Whether you're a novice paddler or an experienced kayaker, the Truckee River offers a variety of paddling experiences, from calm stretches ideal for beginners to challenging rapids for more advanced paddlers. Renting a kayak from local outfitters or bringing your own allows you to explore the river at your own pace, stopping to admire scenic vistas and wildlife along the way.

2. Stand-Up Paddle boarding (SUP): Stand-up paddle boarding has surged in popularity in recent years, and the Truckee River provides an ideal setting for paddlers to test their skills on the water.

Stand-up paddle boarding offers a unique perspective of the river, allowing participants to glide across its surface while enjoying panoramic views of the surrounding mountains and cityscape. Beginners can start with calm sections of the river near downtown Reno, while more experienced paddlers may venture further upstream to tackle the river's rapids and currents.

Safety Tips and Considerations

- **Wear Personal Flotation Devices (PFDs):** Always wear a properly fitting PFD while participating in water sports on the Truckee River, as conditions can change rapidly, and currents can be unpredictable.
- **Check Water Levels:** Before heading out on the river, check current water levels and weather forecasts to ensure safe conditions for your chosen activity. High water levels can increase the difficulty of rafting and kayaking trips, while low water levels may expose hazards such as rocks and debris.
- **Stay Hydrated:** Bring plenty of water and stay hydrated, especially during hot summer months when temperatures can soar. Consider bringing snacks and

sunscreen to keep energy levels up and protect against sunburn.

- **Know Your Limits:** Choose water sports activities that match your skill level and experience, and never attempt to navigate rapids or challenging sections of the river beyond your abilities.
- **Respect Wildlife and Environment:** Be mindful of your impact on the natural environment and wildlife while enjoying water sports on the Truckee River. Avoid disturbing wildlife, respect designated conservation areas, and pack out all trash and recyclables to leave no trace.

Conclusion

Exploring the Truckee River through water sports offers an unparalleled opportunity to connect with nature, challenge yourself, and create unforgettable memories with friends and family. Whether you're seeking the adrenaline rush of whitewater rafting, the tranquility of a scenic float trip, or the exhilaration of kayaking or stand-up paddle boarding, the Truckee River has something for everyone to enjoy. So grab your paddle, don your PFD, and embark on an adventure along the sparkling waters of the Truckee River, where the beauty of the Sierra Nevada Mountains awaits.

Skiing and snowboarding at nearby resorts (winter season).

The winter season in the Sierra Nevada Mountains brings a blanket of snow and an abundance of opportunities for skiing and snowboarding enthusiasts. With several world-class resorts located within a short drive of Reno, Nevada, winter sports enthusiasts have access to some of the best slopes and terrain parks in the country. Whether you're a seasoned pro or hitting the slopes for the first time, the nearby resorts offer something for everyone to enjoy. Here's a comprehensive guide to skiing and snowboarding at nearby resorts during the winter season:

Choosing the Right Resort

1. Mt. Rose Ski Tahoe: As the closest ski resort to Reno, Mt. Rose Ski Tahoe offers convenient access to a variety of terrain for skiers and snowboarders of all abilities. With over 1,200 acres of skiable terrain, including wide-open groomers, challenging moguls, and thrilling tree runs, Mt. Rose provides an ideal setting for winter sports enthusiasts looking for a day on the slopes. The resort boasts breathtaking views of Lake Tahoe and the surrounding mountains, making it a popular destination for locals and visitors alike.

2. NorthStar California Resort: Located just a short drive from Reno in the scenic Lake Tahoe region, NorthStar California Resort offers a premier skiing and snowboarding experience with over 3,000 acres of terrain to explore. From perfectly groomed runs to challenging steeps and powder-filled glades, NorthStar caters to skiers and riders of all levels. The resort also features a variety of amenities, including upscale dining options, luxury lodging, and a vibrant village atmosphere with shops, restaurants, and entertainment.

3. Squaw Valley Alpine Meadows: Renowned for its challenging terrain, expansive alpine bowls, and Olympic heritage, Squaw Valley Alpine Meadows is a must-visit destination for serious skiers and snowboarders. With over 6,000 skiable acres spread across two mountains, the resort offers endless opportunities for exploration and adventure. From steep chutes and wide-open bowls to perfectly manicured groomers and terrain parks, Squaw Valley Alpine Meadows has something for every skill level and riding style.

Exploring the Slopes

1. Skiing: Whether you're a beginner mastering the basics or an expert carving up the mountain, skiing at nearby resorts offers an exhilarating experience for winter sports enthusiasts of all levels. With a variety of terrain ranging from gentle beginner slopes to challenging expert runs, skiers can enjoy endless thrills and breathtaking views as they carve their way down the mountain.

2. Snowboarding: Snowboarding at nearby resorts provides riders with access to some of the best terrain parks and freestyle features in the region. From tabletop jumps and rails to halfpipes and jib lines, snowboarders can showcase their skills and creativity in a dynamic and exciting environment. Whether you're hitting the park for the first time or perfecting your tricks, the resorts offer terrain parks tailored to riders of all abilities.

Tips for a Memorable Experience

- **Arrive Early:** Beat the crowds and maximize your time on the slopes by arriving early in the day when the lifts first open. This allows you to enjoy fresh tracks and uncrowded runs before the crowds arrive.

- **Dress Appropriately:** Be prepared for changing weather conditions by dressing in layers and wearing waterproof and insulated clothing. Don't forget to protect your extremities with gloves, goggles, and a helmet.

- **Stay Hydrated and Fuel Up:** Skiing and snowboarding are physically demanding activities, so be sure to stay hydrated and fuel up with snacks and water throughout the day. Pack energy-boosting snacks like granola bars, trail mix, and fruit to keep your energy levels up on the mountain.

- **Take Breaks:** Listen to your body and take breaks as needed to rest and recharge. Enjoy a hot cocoa or snack at one of the on-mountain lodges or picnic areas while taking in the stunning mountain views.

- **Know Your Limits:** Ski and ride within your ability level and be aware of your surroundings at all times. Follow posted trail signs and ski area rules to ensure a safe and enjoyable experience for yourself and others.

Conclusion

Skiing and snowboarding at nearby resorts during the winter season offer a thrilling and memorable experience for outdoor enthusiasts of all ages. Whether you're carving down groomed slopes, hitting the terrain park, or exploring powder-filled glades, the Sierra Nevada Mountains provide an idyllic setting for winter sports adventures. So grab your skis or snowboard, hit the slopes, and enjoy an unforgettable day of skiing and riding in the winter wonderland of Reno's nearby resorts.

Chapter 9: Cultural Attractions

Museums, galleries, and cultural centers in Reno.

Reno, Nevada, is not only known for its vibrant casinos and outdoor adventures but also for its rich cultural scene, featuring a diverse array of museums, galleries, and cultural centers. From showcasing local art and history to celebrating the region's heritage and creativity, these institutions offer visitors an opportunity to explore, learn, and engage with the community. Here's a comprehensive guide to the museums, galleries, and cultural centers in Reno:

Exploring Reno's Cultural Scene

1. Nevada Museum of Art: As the only accredited art museum in the state, the Nevada Museum of Art is a cultural hub showcasing a diverse collection of visual art, including contemporary and historic works from Nevada and beyond. The museum's exhibitions highlight the intersection of art, environment, and culture, with a focus on promoting creativity, innovation, and dialogue. Visitors can explore a variety of rotating exhibitions, attend artist talks and lectures, and participate in hands-on art activities and workshops.

2. National Automobile Museum: Located in downtown Reno, the National Automobile Museum is home to one of the most extensive collections of vintage automobiles in the world. Featuring over 200 classic cars dating from the late 19th century to the present day, the museum offers visitors a journey through automotive history. From rare and iconic models to one-of-a-kind custom vehicles, the exhibits showcase the evolution of automotive design, technology, and innovation.

3. Nevada Historical Society: Dedicated to preserving and interpreting Nevada's rich history and heritage, the Nevada Historical Society is a treasure trove of artifacts, documents, and photographs documenting the state's past. The museum's exhibits cover a wide range of topics, including Native American culture, mining and railroad history, pioneer life, and the development of Reno and the surrounding region. Visitors can explore interactive displays, research archives, and attend lectures and educational programs.

4. Sierra Arts Foundation: Promoting arts and culture in the Reno area, the Sierra Arts Foundation is a nonprofit organization dedicated to supporting local artists and arts education initiatives. The foundation operates a gallery space showcasing contemporary artwork by emerging and established artists from the region. In addition to exhibitions, the Sierra Arts Foundation offers a variety of programs and services, including artist residencies, workshops, and community events aimed at fostering creativity and cultural exchange.

5. Terry Lee Wells Nevada Discovery Museum: Designed to inspire curiosity and exploration, the Terry Lee Wells Nevada Discovery Museum (The Discovery) is a hands-on science and technology museum located in downtown Reno. The museum features interactive exhibits and educational programs exploring a wide range of topics, including earth sciences, astronomy, physics, and biology. Visitors of all ages can engage in hands-on activities, experiments, and demonstrations, making learning fun and engaging.

6. Artown: Every July, Reno comes alive with Artown, a month-long arts and culture festival celebrating the community's creativity and diversity. Artown features hundreds of events and performances, including live music, dance, theater, visual arts, and cultural exhibitions, held at venues throughout the city. From outdoor concerts and street performances to gallery openings and workshops, Artown offers something for everyone to enjoy, fostering a sense of community and appreciation for the arts.

7. University of Nevada, Reno: Home to a vibrant arts community, the University of Nevada, Reno (UNR) is a hub of cultural activity, featuring galleries, theaters, and performance spaces showcasing the work of students, faculty, and visiting artists. The university's campus is home to the Sheppard Fine Arts Gallery, the Church Fine Arts Building, and the Fleischmann Planetarium and Science Center, offering opportunities for cultural enrichment and creative expression.

Conclusion

Reno's museums, galleries, and cultural centers offer a diverse and enriching experience for visitors and locals alike, showcasing the region's art, history, and heritage. Whether exploring contemporary artwork at the Nevada Museum of Art, delving into automotive history at the National Automobile Museum, or celebrating creativity and innovation at Artown, there's no shortage of cultural attractions to discover in Reno. So immerse yourself in the city's vibrant cultural scene, and uncover the stories, traditions, and creativity that make Reno a unique and dynamic destination

Historic landmarks and sites of interest.

Reno, Nevada, is not only known for its lively casinos and outdoor recreation but also for its rich history and heritage, reflected in its many historic landmarks and sites of interest. From architectural gems to cultural treasures, these sites offer visitors a glimpse into Reno's past and the stories that have shaped the city over the years. Here's a comprehensive guide to the historic landmarks and sites of interest in Reno:

Exploring Reno's Historic Landmarks

1. Lake Mansion: Built-in 1877 by Myron Lake, one of Reno's founding fathers, the Lake Mansion is a historic landmark that serves as a reminder of the city's pioneer days. The mansion, now operated by the Nevada Museum of Art, offers guided tours and exhibits showcasing its rich history and architectural significance. Visitors can explore the beautifully restored interior, featuring period furnishings, artwork, and artifacts, and learn about the prominent figures who once called the mansion home.

2. Virginia Street Bridge: Spanning the Truckee River in downtown Reno, the Virginia Street Bridge is an iconic landmark and a symbol of the city's growth and development. Originally constructed in 1905, the bridge has undergone several renovations over the years but still retains its historic charm and architectural character. Visitors can stroll across the bridge, admire its intricate ironwork and decorative elements, and enjoy panoramic views of the river and surrounding cityscape.

3. Lear Theater: Located in the heart of Reno's Riverwalk District, the Lear Theater is a historic landmark and cultural center that has played a significant role in the city's performing arts scene. Originally built as a church in 1939, the building was later converted into a theater and has since hosted a variety of theatrical productions, concerts, and community events. Today, the Lear Theater continues to serve as a hub for arts and culture, offering performances by local theater groups and visiting artists.

4. Reno Arch: One of the most recognizable landmarks in Reno, the Reno Arch is a symbol of the city's vibrant spirit and welcoming atmosphere. Originally erected in 1926 to promote the Nevada Transcontinental Highway Exposition, the arch has since become an iconic symbol of Reno's gaming and entertainment industry. Visitors can admire the arch's distinctive design and neon lighting, which illuminates the downtown skyline and serves as a backdrop for countless photos and memories.

5. Nevada State Capitol: Located just a short drive from Reno in the nearby city of Carson City, the

Nevada State Capitol is a historic landmark and seat of government for the state of Nevada. Built-in 1871, the Capitol building is a fine example of neoclassical architecture and features a striking silver dome that gleams in the sunlight. Visitors can take guided tours of the Capitol, explore its historic chambers and galleries, and learn about Nevada's political history and legislative process.

6. Fleischmann Planetarium: Situated on the campus of the University of Nevada, Reno, the Fleischmann Planetarium is a historic landmark and educational facility dedicated to astronomy and space science. Built-in 1963, the planetarium was one of the first of its kind in the western United States and has since welcomed millions of visitors from around the world. Visitors can enjoy immersive planetarium shows, interactive exhibits, and stargazing events, learning about the wonders of the universe and our place within it.

7. Reno-Sparks Indian Colony: The Reno-Sparks Indian Colony is a sovereign tribal nation located within the city limits of Reno, Nevada. Established in 1917, the colony is home to members of the Paiute and Shoshone tribes and serves as a center for Native American culture, heritage, and community. Visitors can learn about the history and traditions of the colony through guided tours, cultural exhibits, and events celebrating Native American art, music, and dance.

Conclusion

Reno's historic landmarks and sites of interest offer visitors a fascinating glimpse into the city's past and the events, people, and cultures that have shaped its history. Whether exploring the elegant architecture of the Lake Mansion, strolling across the iconic Virginia Street Bridge, or marveling at the neon glow of the Reno Arch, there's no shortage of historic treasures to discover in Reno. So take a step back in time and uncover the stories and legacies that continue to enrich the fabric of this vibrant and dynamic city.

Cultural events and activities celebrating Reno's heritage.

Reno, Nevada, is a city rich in culture and heritage, boasting a diverse array of events and activities that celebrate its unique identity and history. From traditional festivals and cultural performances to educational workshops and heritage tours, these events offer residents and visitors alike an opportunity to connect with Reno's past, present, and future. Here's a comprehensive guide to the cultural events and activities that celebrate Reno's heritage:

Celebrating Reno's Heritage

1. Reno Rodeo: One of the oldest and most beloved events in Reno, the Reno Rodeo is a celebration of the city's Western heritage and cowboy culture. Held annually in June, the rodeo features a variety of rodeo events, including bull riding, barrel racing, and roping competitions, as well as carnival rides, live music, and food vendors. Visitors can experience the thrill of the rodeo firsthand and immerse themselves in the rich traditions of the American West.

2. Basque Festival: Reno has a strong Basque community, and the annual Basque Festival celebrates the culture, cuisine, and traditions of the Basque people. Held in July, the festival features traditional Basque music and dance performances, as well as food booths offering authentic Basque dishes such as paella, chorizo, and pintxos. Visitors can also participate in Basque-themed activities and learn about the history and heritage of the Basque community in Reno.

3. Artown: Artown is a month-long arts and culture festival held annually in July, showcasing the vibrant creativity and diversity of Reno's cultural scene. The festival features a wide range of events and activities, including live music concerts, dance performances, theater productions, visual art exhibits, and workshops. Visitors can explore different aspects of Reno's cultural heritage through the festival's programming, which highlights local artists, traditions, and stories.

4. Nevada Day Parade: Held every October, Nevada Day celebrates the state's admission to the Union on October 31, 1864, with a parade and other festivities. The Nevada Day Parade features colorful floats, marching bands, equestrian units, and historical reenactments, paying tribute to Nevada's rich history and heritage. Visitors can join in the celebration and experience the excitement of this annual tradition, which brings together residents from across the state to honor their shared heritage.

5. Native American Powwows: Reno is located in the traditional territory of several Native American tribes, and the city hosts a number of Native American powwows and cultural events throughout the year. Powwows are gatherings that celebrate Native American culture through music, dance, storytelling, and arts and crafts. Visitors can experience the beauty and diversity of Native American traditions at these events, which often feature drum circles, traditional regalia, and performances by dancers of all ages.

6. Historic Walking Tours: For those interested in exploring Reno's heritage in a more intimate setting, historic walking tours offer a unique opportunity to learn about the city's past while strolling through its historic neighborhoods and landmarks. Guided tours led by knowledgeable local guides highlight significant sites and buildings, providing insights into Reno's history, architecture, and cultural heritage. Visitors can discover hidden gems and fascinating stories as they walk in the footsteps of early settlers and pioneers.

Conclusion

Reno's cultural events and activities celebrating its heritage offer a glimpse into the city's rich history, traditions, and community spirit. Whether attending the Reno Rodeo, sampling Basque cuisine at the Basque Festival, or exploring the arts and culture of Artown, there's something for everyone to enjoy and appreciate. These events not only showcase Reno's cultural diversity but also foster a sense of pride and connection among residents, preserving and honoring the city's heritage for generations to come. So come and experience the vibrant tapestry of Reno's cultural landscape, and discover the stories and traditions that make this city truly unique.

Chapter 10: Practical Information

Safety tips for travelers

Traveling to Reno, Nevada, can be an exciting and enjoyable experience, but it's essential to prioritize safety to ensure a smooth and worry-free trip. Here are some safety tips for travelers visiting Reno: **1. Stay Informed:** Before your trip, research the current safety situation in Reno and stay updated on any travel advisories or warnings issued by local authorities. Familiarize yourself with the emergency procedures and contact information for local law enforcement, medical facilities, and your country's embassy or consulate.

2. Secure Your Belongings: Keep your belongings secure at all times, especially in crowded areas, tourist attractions, and public transportation. Use a money belt or hidden pouch to carry valuables such as cash, credit cards, and passports, and avoid displaying expensive items or flashy jewelry that may attract attention.

3. Be Vigilant: Stay alert and aware of your surroundings, particularly in unfamiliar or high-traffic areas. Avoid walking alone at night, especially in dimly lit or secluded areas, and trust your instincts if you feel unsafe or uncomfortable. Stick to well-lit streets and populated areas, and consider using transportation services like taxis or ridesharing apps for added safety.

4. Practice Caution in Casinos: If you plan to visit Reno's famous casinos, exercise caution and be mindful of your surroundings. Keep track of your belongings, including purses, wallets, and electronic devices, and avoid leaving them unattended or in plain sight. Be wary of individuals who may approach you with unsolicited offers or invitations, and never share personal or financial information with strangers.

5. Drink Responsibly: If you choose to consume alcohol during your visit to Reno, do so responsibly and in moderation. Avoid excessive drinking, especially if you are unfamiliar with your surroundings or traveling alone. Always keep an eye on your drink and never accept beverages from strangers. If you feel intoxicated or unwell, seek assistance from a trusted friend, bartender, or security personnel.

6. Practice Safe Driving: If you plan to rent a car or drive in Reno, familiarize yourself with local traffic laws and regulations. Observe speed limits, use seat belts, and avoid distracted driving behaviors such as texting or using a handheld device while behind the wheel. Be mindful of road conditions, especially during inclement weather or in mountainous areas, and exercise caution when navigating unfamiliar roads.

7. Protect Against Outdoor Hazards: When exploring Reno's outdoor attractions, such as hiking trails, parks, and natural areas, take precautions to protect yourself against potential hazards. Wear appropriate clothing and footwear for the terrain and weather conditions, stay hydrated, and carry essential supplies such as water, snacks, a map, and a first-aid kit. Be aware of wildlife encounters and adhere to park regulations and guidelines.

8. Trust Your Instincts: Above all, trust your instincts and prioritize your safety and well-being during your time in Reno. If something feels wrong or unsafe, don't hesitate to remove yourself from the situation and seek assistance from local authorities or trusted individuals. By staying vigilant, informed, and prepared, you can enjoy a safe and memorable trip to Reno.

Conclusion

By following these safety tips for travelers, you can ensure a safe and enjoyable experience during your visit to Reno, Nevada. Whether exploring the city's vibrant downtown area, enjoying outdoor adventures in the surrounding natural landscapes, or trying your luck at the casinos, prioritizing safety will help you make the most of your time in this dynamic destination.

Currency and payment methods.

In Reno, Nevada, the primary currency used is the United States Dollar (USD). When traveling to Reno, it's essential to have some cash on hand for small purchases and transactions, as well as to tip service providers such as waitstaff, taxi drivers, and hotel staff.

Payment Methods:

Cash: Cash is widely accepted in Reno and is the most convenient payment method for small purchases, such as meals at local restaurants, souvenirs, and transportation fares. ATMs are readily available throughout the city, allowing travelers to withdraw cash as needed.

Credit and Debit Cards: Major credit and debit cards, including Visa, Mastercard, American Express, and Discover, are widely accepted in Reno, especially at hotels, restaurants, shops, and tourist attractions. However, it's advisable to carry multiple cards from different issuers as a backup in case of any issues with one card.

Mobile Payments: Many businesses in Reno accept mobile payment options such as Apple Pay, Google Pay, and Samsung Pay. These convenient and secure payment methods allow travelers to make purchases using their smartphones or other mobile devices linked to their bank accounts or credit cards.

Traveler's Checks: While traveler's checks were once a popular form of payment for international travelers, they are less commonly used today due to the widespread acceptance of credit and debit cards. However, some hotels and businesses in Reno may still accept traveler's checks, although they may require identification and may charge a fee for processing.

Currency Exchange: If you need to exchange currency during your visit to Reno, currency exchange services are available at some banks, currency exchange offices, and airports. However, it's often more convenient to withdraw cash from ATMs using your debit card, as you'll typically receive a more favorable exchange rate.

Tips for Currency and Payment:

- Inform your bank or credit card company of your travel plans before departing to prevent any issues with card usage due to security measures.
- Carry small denominations of cash for convenience, as some businesses may have limited change available for larger bills.
- Be cautious when using ATMs, especially those located in tourist areas, and avoid using ATMs in isolated or poorly lit areas.
- Keep receipts for all card transactions and monitor your account statements regularly

for any unauthorized charges or discrepancies.

- Consider using a money belt or concealed wallet to keep your cash, cards, and other valuables secure while exploring Reno.

By familiarizing yourself with the currency and payment methods available in Reno and taking precautions to protect your finances and personal information, you can enjoy a hassle-free and convenient shopping and dining experience during your visit to this vibrant city.

Language spoken and cultural etiquette.

In Reno, Nevada, the primary language spoken is English. However, due to its diverse population and status as a popular tourist destination, you may encounter people speaking other languages, especially in areas frequented by tourists. While English is widely understood and spoken, it's always appreciated to learn a few basic phrases in the local language when traveling to any destination.

Cultural Etiquette:

Greetings: When meeting someone for the first time or entering a business establishment, it's customary to greet others with a handshake and a friendly smile. Maintaining eye contact during conversations is considered polite and respectful.

Respect for Diversity: Reno is known for its cultural diversity, and residents take pride in their inclusive and welcoming community. Show respect for different cultures, beliefs, and lifestyles, and avoid making assumptions or judgments based on stereotypes.

Tipping: Tipping is a common practice in Reno, and it's customary to leave a gratuity for service providers such as waitstaff, bartenders, taxi drivers, and hotel housekeeping staff. The standard tipping rate is around 15-20% of the total bill, although this may vary depending on the level of service received.

Personal Space: Americans generally value their personal space and may feel uncomfortable with excessive physical contact, such as hugs or kisses on the cheek, from people they don't know well. Respect others' personal boundaries and avoid invading their space without permission.

Dining Etiquette: When dining out in Reno, it's customary to wait to be seated by a host or hostess and to hold the door open for others as a sign of courtesy. While dining, keep your elbows off the table, chew with your mouth closed, and wait until everyone at the table has been served before beginning to eat.

Punctuality: Being punctual is highly valued in American culture, so it's important to arrive on time for appointments, meetings, and social gatherings. If you anticipate being late, it's polite to call ahead and inform the other party of your estimated arrival time.

Dress Code: Reno has a relatively casual dress code, but attire may vary depending on the occasion and venue. In general, dress modestly and appropriately for the setting, whether it's a casual outing, a business meeting, or a formal event.

Respect for Nature: Reno is surrounded by stunning natural landscapes, including the Sierra Nevada mountains and the Truckee River. Show respect for the environment by disposing of trash properly, staying on designated trails when hiking, and avoiding activities that may harm local wildlife or ecosystems.

By familiarizing yourself with the language spoken and cultural etiquette in Reno, you can show respect for the local customs and traditions and enhance your overall travel experience in this vibrant city.

Conclusion

As we conclude our journey through the vibrant city of Reno, Nevada, it's evident that this destination offers a wealth of experiences for travelers of all interests and preferences. From its rich cultural heritage and diverse culinary scene to its stunning natural landscapes and exciting outdoor adventures, Reno truly has something for everyone.

Throughout this guidebook, we've explored the city's must-see attractions, outdoor activities, entertainment options, dining experiences, and cultural events, providing travelers with valuable insights and recommendations to make the most of their visit.

Whether you're seeking adrenaline-pumping adventures on the slopes of the Sierra Nevada mountains, immersing yourself in the arts and culture of downtown Reno, or simply indulging in the city's world-class dining and entertainment offerings, Reno promises an unforgettable journey filled with excitement, discovery, and memorable moments.

As you embark on your own Reno adventure, may this guidebook serve as your trusted companion, offering inspiration, guidance, and insider tips to ensure a rewarding and unforgettable travel experience in the "Biggest Little City in the World."

ABOUT THE AUTHOR

Meet Marvin Jackson, a seasoned travel guide writer

with a passion for exploration and discovery. As an American hailing from the diverse landscapes of the United States, Marvin has always been drawn to the allure of distant shores and vibrant cultures. With years of experience traversing the globe, Marvin has honed his skills in capturing the essence of each destination he encounters.

Marvin's writing style is characterized by vivid descriptions that transport readers to far-off places, allowing them to immerse themselves in the sights, sounds, and flavors of each locale. His keen eye for detail and insatiable curiosity drive him to uncover hidden gems and share insider tips with fellow travelers.

Through his writing, Marvin seeks to inspire others to embark on their own journeys of discovery, fostering a deeper appreciation for the world's rich tapestry of cultures and landscapes. Join Marvin Jackson on an unforgettable adventure as he guides you through the enchanting landscapes and vibrant cultures of the world.